Research Methodology for Social Sciences

RESEARCH METHODOLOGY for Social Sciences

By

M. Thamilarasan,
Assistant Professor,
Department of Sociology,
University of Madras, Chennai

New Century Publications
New Delhi, India

NEW CENTURY PUBLICATIONS
4800/24, Bharat Ram Road,
Ansari Road, Daryaganj,
New Delhi - 110 002 (India)

Tel.: 011-2324 7798, 4358 7398, 6539 6605
Fax: 011-4101 7798
E-mail: indiatax@vsnl.com • info@newcenturypublications.com
www.newcenturypublications.com

Editorial office:
LG–7, Aakarshan Bhawan,
4754-57/23, Ansari Road, Daryaganj,
New Delhi – 110 002

Tel.: 011-4356 0919

First Published: **2015**

ISBN: **978-81-7708-398-9**

Published by New Century Publications and printed at Salasar Imaging Systems, New Delhi.

Designs: Patch Creative Unit, New Delhi.

PRINTED IN INDIA

About the Book

Research refers to scientific and systematic search for pertinent information on a specific topic. Research comprises defining and redefining problems; formulating hypotheses; collecting, organizing and evaluating data; making deductions; reaching conclusions; and finally suggesting solutions. Research is, thus, an original contribution to the existing stock of knowledge making for its advancement. It is the pursuit of truth with the help of study, observation, comparison and experiment.

Society is an organized group of persons associated together with shared objectives, norms and values. Social research is a systematized investigation to gain new knowledge about social phenomena and problems. Social research helps to analyze and understand human behaviour which forms the basis for all decisions and policies. In social research, society is the laboratory and human beings are the objects. In spite of complexity of human behaviour and human relations, it is possible to find general patterns of social behaviour and thus to make reasonable predictions.

This book ties together the two domains of knowledge, namely qualitative and quantitative research techniques. It is designed to invoke methodological thinking among budding scholars, faculties and researchers in social sciences.

About the Author

M. Thamilarasan is Assistant Professor, Department of Sociology, University of Madras, Chennai. He is a renowned sociologist-cum-social development analyst by profession. He has worked among tribes, peasants, marginalized and aged groups of Tamil Nadu over a period of 15 years.

He received a Centrally-administered Doctoral Fellowship from Indian Council of Social Science Research (ICSSR), New Delhi in 2002 for his doctoral work on Toda Tribal Health in Nilgiri District of Tamil Nadu. He completed a Major Research Project funded by the University Grants Commission (UGC), New Delhi in 2013.

He participated in an international conference on 'Society and Resource Management' organised by Colorado State University, US during June 4-8, 2013.

Contents

Preface

Research can be defined as an art of scientific investigation. One can also define research as a scientific and systematic search for pertinent information on a specific topic. Research comprises defining and redefining problems; formulating hypothesis; collecting, organizing and evaluating data; making deductions; reaching conclusions; and finally suggesting solutions.

Research is, thus, an original contribution to the existing stock of knowledge making for its advancement. It is the pursuit of truth with the help of study, observation, comparison and experiment.

Society is an organized group of persons associated together with shared objectives, norms and values pertaining to society. Research is systematic and organized effort to investigate a specific problem that needs a solution. It contributes to the general body of knowledge.

Social research is a systematized investigation to gain new knowledge about social phenomena and problems. Social research is a scientific undertaking which by means of logical methods, aim to discover new facts or old facts and to analyze their sequences, interrelationships, casual explanations and natural laws which govern them.

Social research helps to analyze and understand human behaviour which forms the basis for all decisions and policies. In social research, society is the laboratory and human beings are the objects. In spite of complexity of human behaviour and human relations, it is possible to find general patterns of social behaviour and thus to make reasonable predictions. This is because the group behaviour can be predicted to some extent compared to individual behaviour. The social phenomenon is reflected to a large extent by the traditions, customs, and values of the society. By using standardized techniques, it is possible to measure even subjective phenomena in objective terms.

All progress is born of inquiry. Doubt is often better than over confidence, for it leads to inquiry, and inquiry leads to invention Research inculcates scientific and inductive thinking and it promotes the development of logical habits of thinking and organization.

Decision-making may not be a part of research, but research certainly facilitates the decisions of the policy maker. Research has its special significance in solving various operational and planning problems of business and industry. Research is equally important for social scientists in studying social relationships and in seeking answers to various social problems. The researcher who knows how to think methodologically is able to select appropriate methods for their social science research.

This book ties together the two domains of knowledge, namely qualitative and quantitative research techniques. The book, it is hoped, will invoke methodological thinking among budding scholars, faculties and researchers in social sciences.

I take this opportunity to place on record my deep sense of gratitude to the following scholars and colleagues for their help, co-operation and encouragement at various stages of the completion of this work: Dr. R. Shankar, Dr. M. Thavamani, Dr. A. Karuppiah, and Ms. C. Vanlalngilneii. Thanks are also due to my parents and spouse for their moral support and good wishes for my academic pursuits.

Chennai **M. Thamilarasan**

October 2014

1

Social Science Research: An Introduction

1.1 Research and Social Research Defined

Research in common parlance refers to a search for knowledge. One can also define research as a scientific and systematic search for pertinent information on a specific topic. In fact, research is an art of scientific investigation. The Advanced Learner's Dictionary of Current English lays down the meaning of research as "a careful investigation or inquiry especially through search for new facts in any branch of knowledge". Redman and Mory define research as a "systematized effort to gain new knowledge". Some people consider research as a movement, a movement from the known to the unknown. It is actually a voyage of discovery. We all possess the vital instinct of inquisitiveness for, when the unknown confronts us, we wonder and our inquisitiveness makes us probe and attain full and fuller understanding of the unknown. This inquisitiveness is the mother of all knowledge and the method, which man employs for obtaining the knowledge of whatever the unknown, can be termed as research.

Research is an academic activity and as such the term should be used in a technical sense. According to Clifford Woody research comprises defining and redefining problems, formulating hypothesis or suggested solutions; collecting, organizing and evaluating data; making deductions and reaching conclusions; and at last carefully testing the conclusions to determine whether they fit the formulating hypothesis. D. Slesinger and M. Stephenson in the Encyclopaedia of Social Sciences define research as "the manipulation of things, concepts or symbols for the purpose of generalizing to extend, correct or verify knowledge, whether that knowledge aids in construction of theory or in the practice of an art".

Research is, thus, an original contribution to the existing stock of knowledge making for its advancement. It is the pursuit of truth with the help of study, observation, comparison and experiment. In short, the search for knowledge through objective and systematic method of finding solution to a problem is research. The systematic approach concerning generalization and the formulation of a theory is also research. As such the term 'research' refers to the systematic method consisting of enunciating the problem, formulating a hypothesis, collecting the facts or data, analyzing the facts and reaching certain conclusions either in the form of solutions(s) towards the concerned problem or in certain generalizations for some theoretical formulation.

Society is an organized group of persons associated together with shared objective, norms and values pertain to the society. People have social life and social process. Research is systematic and organized effort to investigate a specific problem that needs a solution. It contributes to the general body of knowledge. It also corrects human knowledge. Social research now can be defined as the systematic and objective analysis and recording of controlled observations that may lead to the development of generalization, principles or theories resulting in prediction and possibly ultimate control of events in society. It attempts to answer or solve social problems.

According to C.A. Moser, "Social research is a systematized investigation to gain new knowledge about social phenomenon and problems." According to P.V. Young, "Social research is a scientific undertaking which by means of logical methods, aim to discover new facts or old facts and to analyze their sequences, interrelationships, casual explanations and natural laws which govern them".

1.2 Characteristics of Social Science Research

Whatever may be the types of research works and studies,

one thing that is important is that they all meet on the common ground of scientific method employed by them. One expects scientific research to satisfy the following criteria:

1. The purpose of the research should be clearly defined and common concepts be used.
2. The research procedure used should be described in sufficient detail to permit another researcher to repeat the research for further advancement, keeping the continuity of what has already been attained.
3. The procedural design of the research should be carefully planned to yield results that are as objective as possible.
4. The researcher should report with complete frankness, flaws in procedural design and estimate their effects upon the findings.
5. The analysis of data should be sufficiently adequate to reveal its significance and the methods of analysis used should be appropriate. The validity and reliability of the data should be checked carefully.
6. Conclusions should be confined to those justified by the data of the research and limited to those for which the data provide an adequate basis.
7. Greater confidence in research is warranted if the researcher is experienced, has a good reputation in research and is a person of integrity.
8. It is directed towards the solution of problems. The ultimate goal is to discover cause-and-effect relationship between social problems.
9. It emphasis the development of generalizations, principles or theories that will be helpful in predicting future occurrences.
10. It is based upon observable experience or empirical evidence.
11. It demands accurate observations and description. Researchers may choose from a variety or non-qualitative description of their observations.

12. It involves gathering new data from primary sources or using existence data for new purpose.
13. Although social research activities may at time be somewhat random and unsystematic, it is more often characterized by carefully designed procedure that applies rigorous analysis.
14. It requires expertise. The researcher knows what is already known about the problem and how others have investigated.
15. It strives to the objective and logical applying every possible test to validate the procedure employed, data collected and conclusion reached.
16. It involves the guests for answer to unsolved problems.
17. It is characterized by patient and unhurried activity.

1.3 Qualities of Good Research

We can state the qualities of a good research as under:

- **Good Research is Systematic:** It means that research is structured with specified steps to be taken in a specified sequence in accordance with the well defined set of rules. Systematic characteristic of the research does not rule out creative thinking but it certainly does reject the use of guessing and intuition in arriving at conclusions.
- **Good Research is Logical:** This implies that research is guided by the rules of logical reasoning and the logical process of induction and deduction are of great value in carrying out research. Induction is the process of reasoning from a part to the whole whereas deduction is the process of reasoning from some premise to a conclusion which follows from that very premise. In fact, logical reasoning makes research more meaningful in the context of decision making.
- **Good Research is Empirical:** It implies that research is related basically to one or more aspects of a real situation and deals with concrete data that provides a basis for external validity to research results.

- **Good Research is Replicable:** This characteristic allows research results to be verified by replicating the study and thereby building a sound basis for decisions.

Researcher must expect disappointment and discouragement as they pursue the answer to difficult question. It is carefully recorded and reported. Each important term is defined, limiting factors are recognized, procedures are described in detail, reference are carefully documented, results are objectively recorded and conclusions are presented with scholarly caution and restraint.

- It is interdisciplinary in nature.
- It sometimes requires courage.

1.4 Objectives of Social Science Research

The purpose of research is to discover answers to questions through the application of scientific procedures. The main aim of research is to find out the truth which is hidden and which has not been discovered as yet. Though each research study has its own specific purpose, we may think of research objectives as falling into a number of following broad groupings:

1. To gain familiarity with a phenomenon or to achieve new insights into it (studies with this object in view are termed as *exploratory* or *formulative* research studies).
2. To portray accurately the characteristics of a particular individual, situation or a group (studies with this object in view are known as *descriptive* research studies), i.e., to facilitate the understanding of human behaviour, situation or a group.
3. To identify functional relationship existing in the social phenomena.
4. To determine the frequency with which something occurs or with which it is associated with something else (studies with this object in view are known as *diagnostic* research studies);
5. To standardize the society concept, e.g. culture, struggle,

generation gap, social distance etc.
6. To test a hypothesis of a causal relationship between variables (such studies are known as *hypothesis-testing* research studies).
7. To formulate solution to social problems.
8. To develop social revival plan.

1.5 Motivation in Research

What makes people to undertake research? This is a question of fundamental importance. The possible motives for doing research may be either one or more of the following:

1. Desire to get a research degree along with its consequential benefits.
2. Desire to face the challenge in solving the unsolved problems, i.e., concern over practical problems initiates' research.
3. Desire to get intellectual joy of doing some creative work.
4. Desire to be of service to society.
5. Desire to get respectability.

However, this is not an exhaustive list of factors motivating people to undertake research studies. Many more factors such as directives of government, employment conditions, curiosity about new things, desire to understand causal relationships, social thinking and awakening, and the like may as well motivate (or at times compel) people to perform research operations.

1.6 Significance of Research

"All progress is born of inquiry. Doubt is often better than overconfidence, for it leads to inquiry, and inquiry leads to invention" is a famous Hudson Maxim in context of which the significance of research can well be understood. Increased amounts of research make progress possible.

Research inculcates scientific and inductive thinking and it promotes the development of logical habits of thinking and organization. The role of research in several fields of applied economics, whether related to business or to the economy as a whole, has greatly increased in modern times. The increasingly complex nature of business and government has focused attention on the use of research in solving operational problems. Research, as an aid to economic policy, has gained added importance, both for government and business.

Research provides the basis for nearly all government policies in our economic system.

For instance, government's budgets rest in part on an analysis of the needs and desires of the people and on the availability of revenues to meet these needs. The cost of needs has to be equated to probable revenues and this is a field where research is most needed. Through research we can devise alternative policies and can as well examine the consequences of each of these alternatives.

Decision-making may not be a part of research, but research certainly facilitates the decisions of the policy maker. Government has also to chalk out programmes for dealing with all facets of the country's existence and most of these will be related directly or indirectly to economic conditions. The plight of cultivators, the problems of big and small business and industry, working conditions, trade union activities, the problems of distribution, even the size and nature of defence services are matters requiring research. Thus, research is considered necessary with regard to the allocation of nation's resources.

Another area in government, where research is necessary, is collecting information on the economic and social structure of the nation. Such information indicates what is happening in the economy and what changes are taking place. Collecting such statistical information is by no means a routine task, but it involves a variety of research problems. These days nearly all governments maintain large staff of research technicians or experts to carry on this work. Thus, in the context of government, research as a tool to economic policy has three distinct phases of operation, viz.: (i) investigation of economic structure through continual compilation of facts; (ii) diagnosis of events that are taking place and the analysis of the forces underlying them; and (iii) the prognosis, i.e., the prediction of future developments.

Research has its special significance in solving various operational and planning problems of business and industry. Operations research and market research, along with motivational research, are considered crucial and their results assist, in more than one way, in taking business decisions. Market research is the investigation of the structure and development of a market for the purpose of formulating efficient policies for purchasing, production and sales. Operations research refers to the application of mathematical, logical and analytical techniques to the solution of business problems of cost minimization or of profit maximization or what can be termed as optimization problems. Motivational research of determining why people behave as they do is mainly concerned with market characteristics.

In other words, it is concerned with the determination of motivations underlying the consumer (market) behaviour. All these are of great help to people in business and industry who are responsible for taking business decisions. Research with regard to demand and market factors has great utility in business. Given the knowledge of future demand, it is generally not difficult for a firm, or for an industry to adjust its supply schedule within the limits of its projected capacity. Market analysis has become an integral tool of business policy these days. Business budgeting, which ultimately results in a projected profit and loss account, is based mainly on sales estimates which in turn depend on business research. Once sales forecasting is done, efficient production and investment programmes can be set up around which are grouped the purchasing and financing plans. Research, thus, replaces intuitive business decisions by more logical and scientific decisions.

Research is equally important for social scientists in studying social relationships and in seeking answers to various social problems. It provides the intellectual satisfaction of knowing a few things just for the sake of knowledge and also has practical utility for the social scientist to know for the sake of being able to do something better or in a more efficient manner. Research in social sciences is concerned both with knowledge for its own sake and with knowledge for what it can contribute to practical concerns. "This double emphasis is perhaps especially appropriate in the case of social science. On the one hand, its responsibility as a science is to develop a body of principles that make possible the understanding and prediction of the whole range of human interactions. On the other hand, because of its social orientation, it is increasingly being looked to for practical guidance in solving immediate problems of human relations".

In addition to what has been stated above, the significance of research can also be understood keeping in view the following points:

1. To those students who are to write a master's or Ph.D. thesis, research may mean careerism or a way to attain a high position in the social structure.
2. To professionals in research methodology, research may mean a source of livelihood.
3. To philosophers and thinkers, research may mean the outlet for new ideas and insights.
4. To literary men and women, research may mean the development of new styles and creative work.
5. To analysts and intellectuals, research may mean the generalizations of new theories.

Thus, research is the fountain of knowledge for the sake of knowledge and an important source of providing guidelines for solving different business, governmental and social problems. It is a sort of formal training which enables one to understand the new developments in one's field in a better way.

2

Types and Dimensions of Social Research

2.1 Types of Social Research

Social science research may be classified as follows.

2.1.1 Descriptive vs. Analytical: *Descriptive research* includes surveys and fact-finding enquiries of different kinds. The major purpose of descriptive research is description of the state of affairs as it exists at present. In social science and business research we quite often use the term *ex post facto research* for descriptive research studies. The main characteristic of this method is that the researcher has no control over the variables; he can only report what has happened or what is happening. Most *ex post facto research* projects are used for descriptive studies in which the researcher seeks to measure such items as, for example, frequency of shopping, preferences of people, or similar data. *Ex post facto studies* also include attempts by researchers to discover causes even when they cannot control the variables. The methods of research utilized in descriptive research are survey methods of all kinds, including comparative and correlation methods. In *analytical research*, on the other hand, the researcher has to use facts or information already available, and analyze these to make a critical evaluation of the material.

2.1.2 Applied vs. Fundamental: Research can either be applied (or action) research or fundamental (to basic or pure) research. *Applied research* aims at finding a solution for an immediate problem facing a society or an industrial/business organisation, whereas *fundamental research* is mainly concerned with generalisations and with the formulation of a theory. "Gathering knowledge for knowledge's sake is termed 'pure' or 'basic' research". Research concerning some natural phenomenon or relating to pure mathematics are examples of fundamental research.

Similarly, research studies, concerning human behaviour carried on with a view to make generalisations about human behaviour, are also examples of fundamental research, but research aimed at certain conclusions (say, a solution) facing a concrete social or business problem is an example of applied research. Research to identify social, economic or political trends that may affect a particular institution or the copy research (research to find out whether certain communications will be read and understood) or the marketing research or evaluation research are examples of applied research. Thus, the central aim of applied research is to discover a solution for some pressing practical problem, whereas basic research is directed towards finding information that has a broad base of applications and thus, adds to the already existing organized body of scientific knowledge.

2.1.3 Quantitative vs. Qualitative: Quantitative research is based on the measurement of quantity or amount. It is applicable to phenomena that can be expressed in terms of quantity. Qualitative research, on the other hand, is concerned with qualitative phenomenon, i.e. phenomena relating to or involving quality or kind. For instance, when we are interested in investigating the reasons for human behaviour (i.e. why people think or do certain things), we quite often talk of 'Motivation Research', an important type of qualitative research. This type of research aims at discovering the underlying motives and desires, using in depth interviews for the purpose.

Other techniques of such research are word association tests, sentence completion tests, story completion tests and similar other projective techniques. Attitude or opinion research i.e., research designed to find out how people feel or what they think about a particular subject or institution is also qualitative research. Qualitative research is especially important in the behavioural sciences where the aim is to discover the underlying motives of human behaviour. Through such research we can analyse the various factors which motivate people to behave in a particular manner or which make people like or dislike a particular thing. It may be stated, however, that to apply qualitative research in practice is relatively a difficult job and therefore, while doing such research, one should seek guidance from experimental psychologists.

2.1.4 Conceptual vs. Empirical: Conceptual research is that related to some abstract idea(s) or theory. It is generally used by philosophers and thinkers to develop new concepts or to reinterpret existing ones. On the other hand, empirical research relies on experience or observation alone, often without due regard for system and theory. It is data-based research, coming up with conclusions which are capable of being verified by observation or experiment. We can also call it as experimental type of research. In such a research, it is necessary to get at facts firsthand, at their source, and actively to go about doing certain things to stimulate the production of desired information.

In such a research, the researcher must first provide himself with a working hypothesis or guess as to the probable results. He then works to get enough facts (data) to prove or disprove his hypothesis. He then sets up experimental designs which he thinks will manipulate the persons or the materials concerned so as to bring forth the desired information. Such research is thus characterised by the experimenter's control over the variables under study and his deliberate manipulation of one of them to study its effects. Empirical research is appropriate when proof is sought that certain variables affect other variables in some way. Evidence gathered through experiments or empirical studies is today considered to be the most powerful support possible for a given hypothesis.

2.1.5 Some Other Types of Research: All other types of research are variations of one or more of the above stated approaches, based on either the purpose of research, or the time required to accomplish research, on the environment in which research is done, or on the basis of some other similar factor.

1. Form the point of view of time, we can think of research either as *one-time research* or *longitudinal research.* In the former case the research is confined to a single time-period, whereas in the latter case the research is carried on over several time-periods.
2. Research can be *field-setting research* or *laboratory research* or *simulation research,* depending upon the environment in which it is to be carried out.
3. Research can as well be understood as *clinical or diagnostic research.* Such research follows case-study methods or in-depth approaches to reach the basic causal relations. Such studies usually go deep into the causes of things or events that interest us, using very small samples and very deep probing data gathering devices.
4. The research may be *exploratory* or it may be formalized. The objective of exploratory research is the development of hypotheses rather than their testing, whereas formalized research studies are those with substantial structure and with specific hypotheses to be tested.
5. *Historical research* is that which utilizes historical sources like documents, remains, etc. to study events or ideas of the past, including the philosophy of persons and groups at any remote point of time.
6. Research can also be classified as *conclusion-oriented* and decision-oriented. While doing conclusion-oriented research, a researcher is free to pick up a problem, redesign the enquiry as he proceeds and is prepared to conceptualize as he wishes.
7. Decision-oriented research is always for the need of a decision maker and the researcher in this case is not free to embark upon research according to his own inclination.

Operations research is an example of decision oriented research since it is a scientific method of providing executive departments with a quantitative basis for decisions regarding operations under their control.

2.2 Dimensions of Social Research

The dimensions of research include the distinction between applied and basic research, or how people use research. The next is the purpose of doing research, or the goal of a study.

One way to see the dimensions is as decision points for a researcher when moving from a broad topic to a focused research question to the design of a specific study. Table 2.1 lists the various dimensions of social science research

Table 2.1: Various Dimensions of Social Science Research

Dimension of Research	Major Types
How research is used?	Basic, applied
Purpose of the study	Exploratory, descriptive, explanatory
The way time enters in	Cross-sectional, longitudinal (time series, panel, cohort), case study
Technique for Collecting Data	
For Quantitative data	Experiments, surveys, content analysis, existing statistics studies
For Qualitative data	Field research, historical comparative research

These dimensions of research may be further explained elaborately as follows.

Those who seek an understanding of the fundamental nature of social reality are engaged in basic research. Applied researchers, by contrast, primarily want to apply and tailor knowledge to address a specific practical issue. They want to answer a policy question or solve a pressing social problem.

2.2.1 Basic Research: Basic research advances fundamental knowledge about the social world. It focuses on refuting or supporting theories that explain how the social world operates, what makes things happen, why social relations are a certain way, and why society changes. Basic research is the source of most new scientific ideas and ways of thinking about the world.

It is true that knowledge produced by basic research often lacks practical applications in the short term. Yet, basic research provides a foundation for knowledge and understanding that are generalizable to many policy areas, problems, or areas of study.

Basic research is the source of most of the tools- methods, theories, and ideas that applied researchers use.

2.2.2 Applied Research: Applied researchers conduct a study to address a specific concern or to offer solutions to a problem of their employer, a club or organization they are affiliated with, their community or a social movement to which they are committed.

Applied research means a quick, small scale study that provides practical results that people can use in the short term.

The consumers of applied research findings are practitioners.

A. Types of Applied Research:

(a) Evaluation Research: This type of research is widely used in large bureaucratic organizations to find out whether a program, a new way of doing something, a marketing campaign, a policy, and so forth is effective—in other words, "does it work"?

Most evaluation researchers adopt positivist approach and used cost benefit analysis.

Two types of evaluation research are formative and summative. Formative evaluation is built in monitoring or continuous feedback on a program used for program management. Summative evaluation looks at final program outcomes. Both are usually necessary.

(b) Action Research: Action research is applied research that treats knowledge as a form of power and abolishes the line between research and social action. The researcher tries to advance a cause or improve conditions by expanding public awareness. Applied Researches are explicitly political, not value neutral. Action researchers assume that ordinary people can become aware of conditions and learn to take action that can bring about improvement. Action research is associated with the critical social science approach. It attracts researchers how hold specific perspectives.

(c) Social Impact Assessment Research: Social Impact Assessment research may be part of a larger environmental impact statement require by government agencies. Its purpose is to estimate the likely consequence of a planned change. Such an assessment can be used for planning and making choices among alternative policies.

2.2.3 Tools in Applied Research: Applied researchers use two tools: needs assessment and cost benefit analysis.

A. Need Assessment: In a need assessment, a researcher collects data to determine major needs and their severity. It is often a preliminary step before a government agency or charity decides on a strategy to help people. A researcher may confront dilemmas or difficult issues. One issue is to decide on the group to target for the assessment.

A second issue is that people may not express a need in a way that links it directly to policies or long-term solutions. People often have multiple needs. A needs assessment may generate political controversy or suggest solutions beyond local control.

B. Cost-Benefit Analysis: In cost benefit analysis, the researcher estimates the future costs and benefits of one or several proposed actions and gives them monetary values. Cost benefit analysis appears to be a neutral, rational, and technical decision-making strategy, but it can be controversial. People do not necessary agree on what are positive and negative consequence. People look at cost/benefit differently. Someone's cost maybe other's benefits.

There are two ways to assign monetary value to costs and

benefit: (a) contingency evaluation asks people how much something is worth to them, and (b) actual cost evaluation estimates the actual medical and job loss costs.

A significant issue for cost-benefit analysis is the assumption that everything has a price and that people assign similar valuations.

2.2.4 Purpose of a Study

A. Exploration: The researcher's goal is to formulate more precise questions that future research can answer. Exploratory research may be the first stage in sequence of studies.

A researcher may need to conduct an exploratory study in order to know enough to design and execute a second, more systematic and extensive study. Exploratory research rarely yields definitive answers. It addresses the "what" question. It is difficult to conduct because there are few guidelines to follow. Everything is potentially important, steps are not well defined, and the direction of inquiry changes frequently. Exploratory researchers frequently use qualitative techniques for gathering data and they are less wedded to a specific theory or research question.

B. Description: Description—the researcher presents a picture of the specific details of a situation, social setting, or relationship. Much of the social research found in scholarly journals or used for making policy decisions is descriptive.

The researchers begin with a well defined subject and conducts research to describe it accurately. The outcome of a descriptive study is a detailed picture of the subject. Exploring new issues or explaining shy something happens is less of a concern for descriptive researchers than describing how things are. Descriptive research focuses on "how" and "who" questions. Descriptive researcher use most data gathering techniques—surveys, field research, content analysis, and historical comparative research.

C. Explanation: When you encounter an issue that is already known and have a description of it, you might begin to wonder why things are the way they are. Explanation, the desire to know "why", is the purpose of explanatory research. It builds on exploratory and descriptive research and goes on to identify the reason something occurs. Explanatory research looks for causes and reasons.

2.2.5 Time Dimension in Research: An awareness of the time dimension will help researcher read or conduct research because different research questions or issues incorporate time in different ways. Quantitative research is divided into two groups: a single point in time (cross sectional research) versus multiple time points (longitudinal research). Quantitative research looks at a large group of cases, people, or units and measures a limited number of features.

A case study involves qualitative methods and focuses on one or a few cases during a limited time period. Cross-Sectional Research: In cross-sectional research, researchers observe at one point in time. It is usually the simplest and least costly alternative. Its disadvantage is that it cannot capture social processes or change.

2.2.6 Longitudinal Research: Researcher examines features of people or other units at more than one time. It is usually more complex and costly than cross sectional research but it is more powerful, especially when researchers seek answer to questions about social change.

Three types of longitudinal research are as under:

1. Time series research is a longitudinal study in which the same type of information is collected on a group of people or other units across multiple time periods.
2. The panel study observes exactly the same people, group, or organization across time periods.
3. A cohort analysis observes a category of people who share a similar life experience in a specific time period.

2.2.7 Case Studies: In case study research, the researcher examines, in depth, many features of a few cases over duration of time. A case can be an individual, groups, organizations, movements, events or geographic units. Qualitative and case study research are not identical, but "almost all qualitative research seek to construct representations based on in depth, detailed knowledge of cases". Case studies help researchers connect the micro level, or the actions of individual people, to the macro level, or large scale social structures and process. Case studies are likely to produce the best theory.

2.2.8 Data Collection Technique Used: The techniques are grouped into two categories: quantitative, collecting data in the form of numbers, and qualitative, collecting data in the form of word or pictures.

A. Quantitative Data Experiments: Experimental research uses the logic and principles found in natural science research. Experiments can be conducted in laboratories or in real life. Experiments are most effective for explanatory research. In most experiments, the researcher divides the people being studied into two or more groups. He or she then treats both groups identically, except that one group but not the other is given a condition he or she is interested in: the treatment.

B. Survey: Survey techniques are used in descriptive or explanatory research. A survey researcher asks people questions in written questionnaire or during an interview then record answers.

C. Content Analysis: Content analysis is a technique for examine information, or content, in written or symbolic material. Content analysis is used for exploratory and explanatory research but is most often used in descriptive research.

D. Existing Statistics: In existing statistics research, a researcher locates a source of previously collected information, often the form of government reports or previously conducted survey. He or she then reorganizes or combines the information in new ways to address a research question. The existing quantitative information consists of stored survey or other data that a researcher re-examines using various statistical procedures. This is called secondary analysis research. Existing research is most frequently used for descriptive research.

E. Qualitative Data:

- Field Research: Most field researchers conduct case studies on a small group of people for some length of time.
- Historical Comparative Research: Historical comparative research examines aspects of social life in a past historical era or across different cultures. This kind of research combines theory with data collection.

2.2.9 Other Dimensions of Social Research: These are as under.

A. Nature of the Topic. A research project begins with identification of a specific topic, problem or question, such as identifying the health needs of a particular population group, determining the effect of a treatment on physical performance, developing a measuring tool, solving a public relations problem in an organization, and so on. The nature of the topics forms a dimension that extends from purely physical at one end through biological, behavioural, psychological to social topics at the other end.

B. Scope of Enquiry: Single case vs. sample of a population. In a case study, you solve a local problem by finding out "what happened here". Studying a sample allows you to solve a lot more problems by making inferences about "what happens in general".

C. Mode of Enquiry: Observational vs. interventionist: An observational or descriptive study is one in which you try to find out about something without influencing it in any way. In an intervention or experiment, you characterize changes or differences resulting from some action that you have perpetrated.

D. Methods: Quantitative vs. qualitative. Using quantitative methods, you gather data with an instrument, such as a stopwatch or a structured questionnaire, then quantify relationships between variables derived from the data. With qualitative methods you gather information or themes from texts, conversations or loosely structured interviews, then tell a coherent story.

E. Ideological Stance: Objective vs. subjective. Most researchers assume they can make and share observations about objects, then identify and solve problems related to those objects without disagreement about the nature of meaning or reality. Other researchers place more importance on the subjective nature of meaning and truth. This dimension helps characterize some of the so-called research paradigms, from the objectivity of positivism (the dominant paradigm) through the enigmatic ambivalence of post-structuralism to the subjectivity of interpretivism and grounded theory.

F. Political Stance: Neutral vs. partisan. While most researchers aim to present all sides of an issue impartially, some adopt a partisan or adversarial stance by overtly or covertly selecting evidence and biasing arguments towards a particular point of view, invariably their own. Such value-laden research is the basis of the critical or radical paradigm in social sciences, but it also occurs in the physical and biological sciences.

These six dimensions define a kind of multidimensional space in which a given research project or part of a project is represented by a single point. Some regions of this research space are popular, some are unusual but potentially rewarding, and some are inhospitable.

3

Phases of Social Research

Phases of social research (SR) consist of a series of steps necessary to efficiently carry out research on any social phenomena. These actions are closely related. They can be overlapped. Phases of SR basically refer to scientific research process.

Before embarking on the details of research methodology and techniques, it seems appropriate to present a brief overview of the research process. Research process consists of series of actions or steps necessary to effectively carry out research and the desired sequencing of these steps. Figure 3.1 shows a research process.

Figure 3.1 indicates that the research process consists of a number of closely related activities, as shown through I to VII. But such activities overlap continuously rather than following a strictly prescribed sequence.

At times, the first step determines the nature of the last step to be undertaken. If subsequent procedures have not been taken into account in the early stages, serious difficulties may arise which may even prevent the completion of the study. One should remember that the various steps involved in a research process are not mutually exclusive; nor are they separate and distinct.

They do not necessarily follow each other in any specific order and the researcher has to be constantly anticipating at each step in the research process the requirements of the subsequent steps.

However, the following order concerning various steps provides a useful procedural guideline regarding the research process.

Figure 3.1: The Research Process

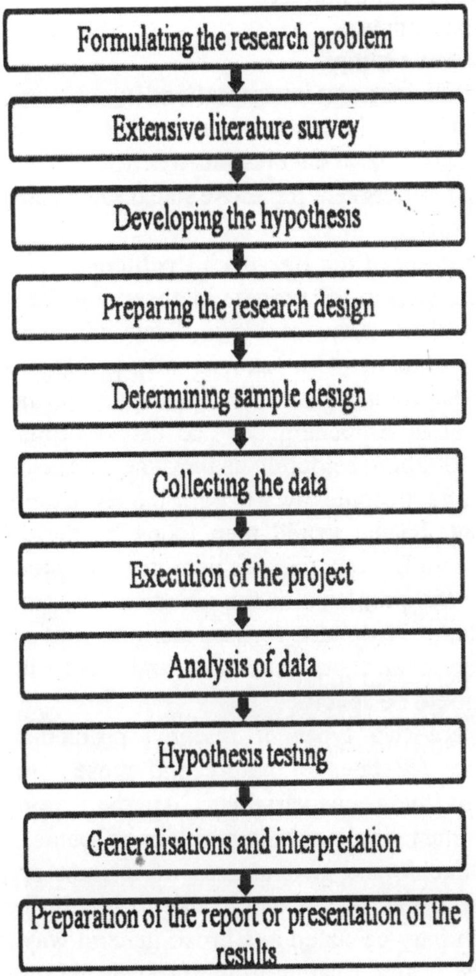

1. Formulation of the research problem.
2. Extensive literature survey.
3. Developing the hypotheses.
4. Preparing the research design.
5. Determining sample design.

6. Collecting the data.
7. Execution of the project.
8. Analysis of data.
9. Hypothesis testing.
10. Generalisations and interpretation.
11. Preparation of the report or presentation of the results, i.e., formal write-up of conclusions reached.

A brief description of the above stated steps will be helpful.

3.1 Formulation of the Research Problem

The first step in SR process is observing the situation and sensing problem. New problems keep on emerging in the social environment. One should sense these development origins in the environment. At this stage, one may not know exactly what is happening but one can definitely sense that things are not going smoothly as they should be.

Once one become aware of what is happening in the environment, he/she would then focus on the problem. The researcher singles out the problem for the study, i.e. what exactly are the problems in the situation. It is thus, problem-defining stage. Without a focused definition of problem, data tends to be irrelevant, expensive and confusing. Research problem should be specific.

There are two types of research problems, viz., those which relate to states of nature and those which relate to relationships between variables. At the very outset, the researcher must single out the problem he wants to study, i.e., one must decide the general area of interest or aspect of a subject-matter that he/she would like to inquire into. Initially, the problem may be stated in a broad general way and then the ambiguities, if any, relating to the problem be resolved. Then, the feasibility of a particular solution has to be considered before a working formulation of the problem can be set up. The formulation of a general topic into a specific research problem, thus, constitutes the first step in a scientific enquiry.

Essentially two steps are involved in formulating the

research problem, viz., understanding the problem thoroughly, and rephrasing the same into meaningful terms from an analytical point of view. The best way of understanding the problem is to discuss it with one's own colleagues or with those having some expertise in the matter. In an academic institution the researcher can seek the help from a guide who is usually an experienced man and has several research problems in mind. Often, the guide puts forth the problem in general terms and it is up to the researcher to narrow it down and phrase the problem in operational terms. In private business units or in governmental organizations, the problem is usually earmarked by the administrative agencies with which the researcher can discuss as to how the problem originally came about and what considerations are involved in its possible solutions.

The researcher must at the same time examine all available literature to get himself acquainted with the selected problem. He/she may review two types of literature—the conceptual literature concerning the concepts and theories, and the empirical literature consisting of studies made earlier which are similar to the one proposed. The basic outcome of this review will be the knowledge as to what data and other materials are available for operational purposes which will enable the researcher to specify his own research problem in a meaningful context.

After this the researcher rephrases the problem into analytical or operational terms i.e., to put the problem in as specific terms as possible. This task of formulating, or defining, a research problem is a step of greatest importance in the entire research process. The problem to be investigated must be defined unambiguously for that will help discriminating relevant data from irrelevant ones. Care must however be taken to verify the objectivity and validity of the background facts concerning the problem.

Professor W.A. Neiswanger correctly states that the statement of the objective is of basic importance because it determines the data which are to be collected, the characteristics of the data which are relevant, relations which are to be explored, the choice of techniques to be used in these explorations and the form of the final report. If there are certain pertinent terms, the same should be clearly defined along with the task of formulating the problem. In fact, formulation of the problem often follows a sequential pattern where a number of formulations are set up, each formulation more specific than the preceding one, each one phrased in more analytical terms, and each more realistic in terms of the available data and resources.

3.2 Extensive Literature Survey

Once the problem is formulated, a brief summary of it should be written down. It is compulsory for a research worker writing a thesis for a Ph.D. degree to write a synopsis of the topic and submit it to the necessary committee or the research board for approval. At this juncture, the researcher should undertake extensive literature survey connected with the problem. For this purpose, the abstracting and indexing journals and published or unpublished bibliographies are the first place to go to.

Academic journals, conference proceedings, government reports, books etc., must be tapped depending on the nature of the problem. In this process, it should be remembered that one source will lead to another. The earlier studies, if any, which are similar to the study in hand, should be carefully studied. A good library will be a great help to the researcher at this stage. This helps to integrate information locally so that reason for the problem can be conceptualized. This helps to develop theoretical framework. This step essentially involves a review of related literature. It familiarizes the researcher with what is already known and what is still unknown and untested.

3.3 Developing the Hypotheses

A hypothesis is a tentative answer to question. It is an educated guess. It is generally based upon prior research. It is subjected to the process of verification or disconfirmation. Hypothesis is conjectured relationship between two or more variables expressed in the form of testable statements.

After extensive literature survey, researcher should state in clear terms the working hypothesis or hypotheses. Working hypothesis is tentative assumption made in order to draw out and test its logical or empirical consequences. As such the manner in which research hypotheses are developed is particularly important since they provide the focal point for research. They also affect the manner in which tests must be conducted in the analysis of data and indirectly the quality of data which is required for the analysis. In most types of research, the development of working hypothesis plays an important role. Hypothesis should be very specific and limited to the piece of research in hand because it has to be tested. The role of the hypothesis is to guide the researcher by delimiting the area of research and to keep him on the right track. It sharpens his thinking and focuses attention on the more important facets of the problem. It also indicates the type of data required and the type of methods of data analysis to be used. How does one go about developing working hypotheses? The answer is by using the following approach:

1. Discussions with colleagues and experts about the problem, its origin and the objectives in seeking a solution;
2. Examination of data and records, if available, concerning the problem for possible trends, peculiarities and other clues;
3. Review of similar studies in the area or of the studies on similar problems; and
4. Exploratory personal investigation which involves original field interviews on a limited scale with interested parties and individuals with a view to secure greater insight into the practical aspects of the problem.

Thus, working hypotheses arise as a result of a-priori thinking about the subject, examination of the available data and material including related studies and the counsel of experts and interested parties. Working hypotheses are more useful when stated in precise and clearly defined terms. It may as well be remembered that occasionally we may encounter a problem where we do not need working hypotheses, especially in the case of exploratory or formulative researches which do not aim at testing the hypothesis. But as a general rule, specification of working hypotheses is another basic step of the research process in most research problems.

3.4 Preparing the Research Design

A research design is the plan, structure and strategy for conducting research. It describes the general framework for collecting, analyzing and evaluating data. It helps to obtain answer to research questions and to control variance. It enables the researcher to answer research questions to validity, objectively, accurately and economically as possible. Design should be carefully worked out to yield dependable and valid answer to the research questions.

The research problem having been formulated in clear cut terms, the researcher will be required to prepare a research design, i.e., he will have to state the conceptual structure within which research would be conducted. The preparation of such a design facilitates research to be as efficient as possible yielding maximal information. In other words, the function of research design is to provide for the collection of relevant evidence with minimal expenditure of effort, time and money. But how all these can be achieved depends mainly on the research purpose.

Research purposes may be grouped into four categories.

1. Exploration.
2. Description.
3. Diagnosis.
4. Experimentation.

A flexible research design which provides opportunity for considering many different aspects of a problem is considered appropriate if the purpose of the research study is that of exploration. But when the purpose happens to be an accurate description of a situation or of an association between variables, the suitable design will be one that minimizes bias and maximizes the reliability of the data collected and analyzed.

There are several research designs, such as, experimental and non-experimental hypothesis testing. Experimental designs can be either informal design (such as before-and-after without control, after-only with control, before-and-after with control) or formal designs (such as completely randomized design, randomized block design, Latin square design, simple and complex factorial designs), out of which the researcher must select one for his own project.

The preparation of the research design, appropriate for a particular research problem, involves usually the consideration of the following:

1. The means of obtaining the information;
2. The availability and skills of the researcher and his staff (if any);
3. Explanation of the way in which selected means of obtaining information will be organized;
4. The reasoning leading to the selection;
5. The time available for research; and
6. The cost factor relating to research, i.e., the finance available for the purpose.

3.5 Determining Sample Design

All the items under consideration in any field of inquiry constitute a *universe* or *population*. A complete enumeration of all the items in the 'population' is known as a census inquiry. It can be presumed that in such an inquiry when all the items are covered no element of chance is left and highest accuracy is obtained. But in practice this may not be true. Even the slightest element of bias in such an inquiry will get larger and larger as the number of observations increases. Moreover, there is no way of checking the element of bias or its extent except through a resurvey or use of sample checks. Besides, this type of inquiry involves a great deal of time, money and energy. Not only this, census inquiry is not possible in practice under many circumstances.

For instance, blood testing is done only on sample basis. Hence, quite often we select only a few items from the universe for our study purposes. The items so selected constitute what is technically called a sample. The researcher must decide the way of selecting a sample or what is popularly known as the sample design. In other words, a sample design is a definite plan determined before any data are actually collected for obtaining a sample from a given population. Thus, the plan to select 12 of a city's 200 drugstores in a certain way constitutes a sample design.

Samples can be either probability samples or non-probability samples. With probability samples each element has a known probability of being included in the sample but the non-probability samples do not allow the researcher to determine this probability. Probability samples are those based on simple random sampling, systematic sampling, stratified sampling, cluster/area sampling whereas non-probability samples are those based on convenience sampling, judgment sampling and quota sampling techniques. A brief mention of the important sample designs is as follows:

3.5.1 Deliberate Sampling: Deliberate sampling is also known as purposive or non-probability sampling. This sampling method involves purposive or deliberate selection of particular units of the universe for constituting a sample which represents the universe. When population elements are selected for inclusion in the sample based on the ease of access, it can be called *convenience sampling*. If a researcher wishes to secure data from, say, gasoline buyers, he may select a fixed number of petrol stations and may conduct interviews at these stations. This would be an example of convenience sample of gasoline buyers. At times, such a procedure may give very biased results particularly when the population is not homogeneous. On the other hand, in *judgement sampling*, the researcher's judgement is used for selecting items which he considers as representative of the population.

For example, a judgement sample of college students might be taken to secure reactions to a new method of teaching. Judgement sampling is used quite frequently in qualitative research where the desire happens to be to develop hypotheses rather than to generalise to larger population.

3.5.2 Simple Random Sampling: This type of sampling is also known as chance sampling or probability sampling where each and every item in the population has an equal chance of inclusion in the sample and each one of the possible samples, in case of finite universe, has the same probability of being selected. For example, if we have to select a sample of 300 items from a universe of 15,000 items, then we can put the names or numbers of all the 15,000 items on slips of paper and conduct a lottery. Using the random number tables is another method of random sampling. To select the sample, each item is assigned a number from 1 to 15,000. Then, 300 five digit random numbers are selected from the table. To do this, we select some random starting point and then a systematic pattern is used in proceeding through the table.

We might start in the 4th row, second column and proceed down the column to the bottom of the table and then move to the top of the next column to the right. When a number exceeds the limit of the numbers in the frame, in our case over 15,000, it is simply passed over and the next number selected that does fall within the relevant range. Since the numbers were placed in the table in a completely random fashion, the resulting sample is random. This procedure gives each item an equal probability of being selected. In case of infinite population, the selection of each item in a random sample is controlled by the same probability and that successive selections are independent of one another.

3.5.3 Systematic Sampling: In some instances the most practical way of sampling is to select every 15th name on a list, every 10th house on one side of a street and so on. Sampling of this type is known as systematic sampling. An element of randomness is usually introduced into this kind of sampling by using random numbers to pick up the unit with which to start. This procedure is useful when sampling frame is available in the form of a list. In such a design the selection process starts by picking some random point in the list and then every *n*th element is selected until the desired number is secured.

3.5.4 Stratified Sampling: If the population from which a sample is to be drawn does not constitute a homogeneous group, then stratified sampling technique is applied so as to obtain a representative sample. In this technique, the population is stratified into a number of non-overlapping subpopulations or strata and sample items are selected from each stratum. If the items selected from each stratum is based on simple random sampling the entire procedure, first stratification and then simple random sampling, is known as *stratified random sampling*.

A. Quota Sampling: In stratified sampling the cost of taking random samples from individual strata is often so expensive that interviewers are simply given quota to be filled from different strata, the actual selection of items for sample being left to the interviewer's judgment. This is called quota sampling. The size of the quota for each stratum is generally proportionate to the size of that stratum in the population. Quota sampling is thus an important form of non-probability sampling. Quota samples generally happen to be judgment samples rather than random samples.

B. Cluster Sampling and Area Sampling: Cluster sampling involves grouping the population and then selecting the groups or the clusters rather than individual elements for inclusion in the sample. Suppose some departmental store wishes to sample its credit card holders. It has issued its cards to 15,000 customers. The sample size is to be kept say 450. For cluster sampling, this list of 15,000 card holders could be formed into 100 clusters of 150 card holders each. Three clusters might then be selected for the sample randomly. The sample size must often be larger than the simple random sample to ensure the same level of accuracy because is cluster sampling procedural potential for order bias and other sources of error are usually accentuated. The clustering approach can, however, make the sampling procedure relatively easier and increase the efficiency of field work, especially in the case of personal interviews.

Area sampling is quite close to cluster sampling and is often talked about when the total geographical area of interest happens to be big one. Under area sampling we first divide the total area into a number of smaller non-overlapping areas, generally called geographical clusters, then a number of these smaller areas are randomly selected, and all units in these small areas are included in the sample. Area sampling is especially helpful where we do not have the list of the population concerned. It also makes the field interviewing more efficient since interviewer can do many interviews at each location.

C. Multi-stage Sampling: This is a further development of the idea of cluster sampling. This technique is meant for big inquiries extending to a considerably large geographical area like an entire country. Under multi-stage sampling, the first stage may be to select large primary sampling units such as states, then districts, then towns and finally certain families within towns. If the technique of random-sampling is applied at all stages, the sampling procedure is described as multi-stage random sampling.

D. Sequential Sampling: This is somewhat a complex sample design where the ultimate size of the sample is not fixed in advance but is determined according to mathematical decisions on the basis of information yielded as the survey progresses. This design is usually adopted under acceptance sampling plan, in the context of statistical quality control.

In practice, several of the methods of sampling described

above may well be used in the same manner so that bias can be eliminated and sampling error can be estimated. But purposive sampling is considered desirable when the universe happens to be small and a known characteristic of it is to be studied intensively. Also, there are conditions under which sample designs other than random sampling may be considered better for reasons like convenience and low costs.

The sample design to be used must be decided by the researcher taking into consideration the nature of the inquiry and other related factors.

3.6 Collecting the Data

In dealing with any real life problem it is often found that data at hand are inadequate, and hence, it becomes necessary to collect data that are appropriate. There are several ways of collecting the appropriate data which differ considerably in context of money costs, time and other resources at the disposal of the researcher.

Primary data can be collected either through experiment or through survey. If the researcher conducts an experiment, he observes some quantitative measurements, or the data, with the help of which he examines the truth contained in his hypothesis. But in the case of a survey, data can be collected by any one or more of the following ways.

3.6.1 By Observation: This method implies the collection of information by way of investigator's own observation, without interviewing the respondents. The information obtained relates to what is currently happening and is not complicated by either the past behaviour or future intentions or attitudes of respondents. This method is no doubt an expensive method and the information provided by this method is also very limited. As such this method is not suitable in inquiries where large samples are concerned.

3.6.2 Through Personal Interview: The investigator follows a rigid procedure and seeks answers to a set of pre-conceived questions through personal interviews. This method of collecting data is usually carried out in a structured way where output depends upon the ability of the interviewer to a large extent.

3.6.3 Through Telephone Interviews: This method of collecting information involves contacting the respondents on telephone itself. This is not a very widely used method but it plays an important role in industrial surveys in developed regions, particularly, when the survey has to be accomplished in a very limited time.

3.6.4 By Mailing of Questionnaires: The researcher and the respondents do come in contact with each other if this method of survey is adopted. Questionnaires are mailed to the respondents with a request to return after completing the same. It is the most extensively used method in various economic and business surveys. Before applying this method, usually a pilot study for testing the questionnaire is conduced which reveals the weaknesses, if any, of the questionnaire. Questionnaire to be used must be prepared very carefully so that it may prove to be effective in collecting the relevant information.

3.6.5 Through Schedules: Under this method the enumerators are appointed and given training. They are provided with schedules containing relevant questions. These enumerators go to respondents with these schedules. Data is collected by filling up the schedules by enumerators on the basis of replies given by respondents. Much depends upon the capability of enumerators so far as this method is concerned. Some occasional field checks on the work of the enumerators may ensure sincere work.

The researcher should select one of these methods of collecting the data taking into consideration the nature of investigation, objective and scope of the inquiry, financial resources, available time and the desired degree of accuracy. Though he should pay attention to all these factors but much depends upon the ability and experience of the researcher.

In this context, A.L. Bowley very aptly remarks, that in

collection of statistical data, commonsense is the chief requisite and experience the chief teacher.

3.7 Execution of the Project

Execution of the project is a very important step in the research process. If the execution of the project proceeds on correct lines, the data to be collected would be adequate and dependable. The researcher should see that the project is executed in a systematic manner and in time. If the survey is to be conducted by means of structured questionnaires, data can be readily machine-processed. In such a situation, questions as well as the possible answers may be coded. If the data are to be collected through interviewers, arrangements should be made for proper selection and training of the interviewers. The training may be given with the help of instruction manuals which explain clearly the job of the interviewers at each step. Occasional field checks should be made to ensure that the interviewers are doing their assigned job sincerely and efficiently.

A careful watch should be kept for unanticipated factors in order to keep the survey as much realistic as possible. This, in other words, means that steps should be taken to ensure that the survey is under statistical control so that the collected information is in accordance with the pre-defined standard of accuracy. If some of the respondents do not cooperate, some suitable methods should be designed to tackle this problem. One method of dealing with the non-response problem is to make a list of the non-respondents and take a small sub-sample of them, and then with the help of experts vigorous efforts can be made for securing response.

3.8 Analysis of Data

After the data have been collected, the researcher turns to the task of analyzing them. The analysis of data requires a number of closely related operations such as establishment of categories, the application of these categories to raw data through coding, tabulation and then drawing statistical inferences. The unwieldy data should necessarily be condensed into a few manageable groups and tables for further analysis. Thus, researcher should classify the raw data into some purposeful and usable categories.

Coding operation is usually done at this stage through which the categories of data are transformed into symbols that may be tabulated and counted.

Editing is the procedure that improves the quality of the data for coding. With coding the stage is ready for tabulation.

Tabulation is a part of the technical procedure wherein the classified data are put in the form of tables. The mechanical devices can be made use of at this juncture. A great deal of data, especially in large inquiries, is tabulated by computers. Computers not only save time but also make it possible to study large number of variables affecting a problem simultaneously.

Analysis work after tabulation is generally based on the computation of various percentages, coefficients, etc., by applying various well defined statistical formulae. In the process of analysis, relationships or differences supporting or conflicting with original or new hypotheses should be subjected to tests of significance to determine with what validity data can be said to indicate any conclusion(s).

For instance, if there are two samples of weekly wages, each sample being drawn from factories in different parts of the same city, giving two different mean values, then our problem may be whether the two mean values are significantly different or the difference is just a matter of chance. Through the use of statistical tests, we can establish whether such a difference is a real one or is the result of random fluctuations. If the difference happens to be real, the inference will be that the two samples come from different universes and if the difference is due to chance, the conclusion would be that the two samples belong to the same universe.

Similarly, the technique of analysis of variance can help us in analyzing whether three or more varieties of seeds grown on certain fields yield significantly different results or not. In brief, the researcher can analyze the collected data with the help of various statistical measures. The purpose is to reduce data to intelligible and interpretable form so that elations of research problem can be studied and tested.

3.9 Hypothesis Testing

After analyzing the data as stated above, the researcher is in a position to test the hypotheses, if any, he had formulated earlier. Do the facts support the hypotheses or they happen to be contrary? This is the usual question which should be answered while testing hypotheses.

Various tests, such as Chi square test, *t*-test, *F*-test, have been developed by statisticians for the purpose. The hypotheses may be tested through the use of one or more of such tests, depending upon the nature and object of research inquiry. Hypothesis testing will result in either accepting the hypothesis or in rejecting it. If the researcher had no hypotheses to start with, generalizations established on the basis of data may be stated as hypotheses to be tested by subsequent researches in times to come.

3.10 Generalization and Interpretation

Interpretation takes the result of data analysis, makes inference pertinent to the research relation studied and draws conclusion about the relations. Generalization is the act of giving general form to these conclusions.

If a hypothesis is tested and upheld several times, it may be possible for the researcher to arrive at generalization, i.e., to build a theory. As a matter of fact, the real value of research lies in its ability to arrive at certain generalizations. If the researcher had no hypothesis to start with, he might seek to explain his findings on the basis of some theory. It is known as interpretation. The process of interpretation may quite often trigger off new questions which in turn may lead to further researches.

3.11 Preparation of the Report or the Thesis

Finally, the researcher has to prepare the report of what has been done by him. Writing of report must be done with great care keeping in view the following.

1. Layout of the report should be as follows:
   (a) Preliminary pages,
   (b) Main text, and
   (c) End matter.

In the preliminary pages, the report should carry title and date followed by acknowledgements and foreword. Then there should be a table of contents followed by a list of tables and list of graphs and charts, if any, given in the report.

The main text of the report should have the following parts:

1. **Introduction:** It should contain a clear statement of the objective of the research and an explanation of the methodology adopted in accomplishing the research. The scope of the study along with various limitations should as well be stated in this part.
2. **Summary of Findings:** After introduction there would appear a statement of findings and recommendations in non-technical language. If the findings are extensive, they should be summarized.
3. **Main Report:** The main body of the report should be presented in logical sequence and broken-down into readily identifiable sections.
4. **Conclusion:** Towards the end of the main text, researcher should again put down the results of his research clearly and precisely. In fact, it is the final summing up.

At the end of the report, appendices should be enlisted in respect of all technical data. Bibliography, i.e., list of books, journals, reports, etc., consulted, should also be given in the end. Index should also be given specially in a published research report.

1. Report should be written in a concise and objective style in simple language avoiding vague expressions such as 'it

seems,' 'there may be', and the like.

2. Charts and illustrations in the main report should be used only if they present the information more clearly and forcibly. Calculated 'confidence limits' must be mentioned and the various constraints experienced in conducting research operations may as well be stated.

The objective of writing a report is to tell readers the problems investigated, the method used to solve problems, result of the investigation and the conclusion from the result.

4

Research and Scientific Methods

For a clear perception of the term research, one should know the meaning of scientific method. The two terms, research and scientific method, are closely related. Research, as we have already stated, can be termed as "an inquiry into the nature of, the reasons for, and the consequences of any particular set of circumstances, whether these circumstances are experimentally controlled or recorded just as they occur. Further, research implies the researcher is interested in more than particular results; he is interested in the repeatability of the results and in their extension to more complicated and general situations".

On the other hand, the philosophy common to all research methods and techniques, although they may vary considerably from one science to another, is usually given the name of scientific method. In this context, Karl Pearson writes, "The scientific method is one and same in the branches (of science) and that method is the method of all logically trained minds... the unity of all sciences consists alone in its methods, not its material; the man who classifies facts of any kind whatever, who sees their mutual relation and describes their sequences, is applying the scientific method and is a man of science". Scientific method is the pursuit of truth as determined by logical considerations. The ideal of science is to achieve a systematic interrelation of facts. Scientific method attempts to achieve "this ideal by experimentation, observation, logical arguments from accepted postulates and a combination of these three in varying proportions". In scientific method, logic aids in formulating propositions explicitly and accurately so that their possible alternatives become clear.

Further, logic develops the consequences of such alternatives, and when these are compared with observable phenomena, it becomes possible for the researcher or the scientist to state which alternative is most in harmony with the observed facts. All this is done through experimentation and survey investigations which constitute the integral parts of scientific method. Experimentation is done to test hypotheses and to discover new relationships, if any, among variables. But the conclusions drawn on the basis of experimental data are generally criticized for faulty assumptions, poorly designed experiments, badly executed experiments or faulty interpretations. As such the researcher must pay all possible attention while developing the experimental design and must state only probable inferences. The purpose of survey investigations may also be to provide scientifically gathered information to work as a basis for the researchers for their conclusions.

The scientific method is, thus, based on certain basic postulates which can be stated as under:

1. It relies on empirical evidence;
2. It utilizes relevant concepts;
3. It is committed to only objective considerations;
4. It presupposes ethical neutrality, i.e. it aims at nothing but making only adequate and correct statements about population objects;
5. It results into probabilistic predictions;
6. Its methodology is made known to all concerned for critical scrutiny is for use in testing the conclusions through replication; and
7. It aims at formulating most general axioms or what can be termed as scientific theories.

Thus, "the scientific method encourages a rigorous, impersonal mode of procedure dictated by the demands of logic and objective procedure". Accordingly, scientific method implies an objective, logical and systematic method, i.e., a method free from personal bias or prejudice, a method to ascertain demonstrable qualities of a phenomenon capable of being verified, a method wherein the researcher is guided by the rules of logical reasoning, a method wherein the investigation proceeds in an orderly manner and a method that implies internal consistency.

4.1 Relationship between Theory and Research

Theory plays a dual role in research. On the one hand, new theories solve research problems by accounting for unexplained phenomena and by superseding questionable older theories. On the other hand, existing theory guides researchers in formulating research problems. In determining whether and in what respects a phenomenon or a theory is problematic, researchers consider the context of accumulated theoretical as well as empirical knowledge. And only those phenomena and theories that appear to be problematic when viewed in that context are then studied. Ideally, at least, formulating problems in this manner ensures the orderly advance of knowledge because new research is aimed at solving problems left unsolved in past work rather than being aimed at either totally new or theoretically irrelevant problems.

The guiding role of theory in problem formulation is obvious in verificational studies. But while less obvious, it is equally important in exploratory research. To a large degree, pre-existing theories define both the territory to be explored in the search for problems, and the nature of the new facts one hopes to discover. Of course, opinions differ about how explicit the theoretical background of exploratory research should be. Some recommend spelling it out in nearly as much detail as in verification research, stating exactly what existing theory leads you to expect and why. Others object to granting existing theory such a directive role and prefer instead to work with general theoretical orientations that sensitize the investigator to important but less precise categories of data. Closure in either the definition of concepts or the statement of hypotheses is avoided in favour of more open "sensitizing concepts" and the "suspension of expectations".

In the first view, new problems and hypotheses emerge from the confrontation between old theories and new data, much as in verification. In the second view, new problems and hypotheses emerge from the confrontation between the data and a theoretically oriented and sensitized investigator.

Theory development relies on research, and research relies on theory. Brown (1977) characterized the relationship between theory and research as dialectic, a transaction whereby theory determines what data are to be collected and research findings provide challenges to accepted theories.

Research, then, is neither nor less than the vehicle for theory development. It is the method used to gather the data for the theory. This is true whether the purpose of the research is to generate a theory or to test one. When the purpose is theory generation, the phenomenon of interest suggests things to look for. For example, if a theory of clients' perceptions of factors influencing their adherence to a nursing care plan were to be generated, one source of data would be clients' perceptions of why they were willing and able to follow the care plan. Conversely, if the purpose is theory testing, the theory dictates the data to be collected. For example, if a theory proposes that emotional support provided by spouses is the best predictor of clients' adherence to nursing care plans, then the data to be collected include the extent of emotional support provided by spouses and the extent to which clients adhere to care plans.

4.2 Types of Theory and Research

The relationship between theory and research can be further explained by exploring the research designs used to develop various types of theories. Theories generally are classified as descriptive, relational, or explanatory. The research designs that generate and test these types of theories are, respectively, descriptive, correlation, and experimental.

4.2.1 Descriptive Theory and Descriptive Research: Descriptive theories are the most basic type of theory. They describe or classify specific dimensions or characteristics of individuals, groups, situations, or events by summarizing the commonalities found in discrete observations. They state "what is". Descriptive theories are needed when nothing or very little is known about the phenomenon in question.

There are two categories of descriptive theories: naming and classification (Stevens, 1984). A naming theory is a description of the dimensions or characteristics of some phenomenon. A classification theory is more elaborate in that it states that the dimensions or characteristics of a given phenomenon are structurally inter-related. The dimensions may be mutually exclusive, overlapping, hierarchical, or sequential. Classification theories frequently are referred to as typologies or taxonomies.

Descriptive theories are generated and tested by descriptive research. This type of research is also called exploratory research. Descriptive research may or may not use empirical method.

The method of grounded theory yields a description process occurring in social situations. Every piece of data is compared with every other piece in order to discover the dominant social processes that characterize the phenomenon under study.

4.2.2 Relational Theories and Correlation Research: Relational theories specify relations between dimensions or characteristics of individuals, groups, situations, or events. They explain how the parts of a phenomenon are related to one another. These theories can be developed only after the essential characteristics of a phenomenon are known, that is, only after descriptive theories have been developed and validated.

4.2.3 Explanatory Theory and Experimental Research: Explanatory theories move beyond relational statements to the prediction of precise causative relationships between dimensions or characteristics of a phenomenon or differences between groups. This type of theory addresses cause and effect, the "why" of changes in a phenomenon. Explanatory theories may be developed after relational theories have been formulated.

4.3 Decentralized Theorizing and Cumulative Knowledge

In contrast with an earlier time, when Glaser and Strauss

(1967) criticized the overemphasis on verification in social research, many social scientists now do their own theorizing in the course of their research, rather than testing others' theories. As Freese (1972) has suggested with respect to sociology, there is now widespread acceptance of two premises.

1. Sociological investigations should consist of constructing and testing theories; and
2. Theory construction is not the exclusive province of the intellectual elite, but is the proper responsibility of each sociologist when he defines some social phenomenon as problematic".

If individual researchers are to be their own theoreticians, however, then each must also accept some responsibility for synthesis; otherwise, we risk inundation by idiosyncratic theories that may be firmly grounded in their authors' research but that are of problematic significance in the larger scheme of things. Verification research which by its very nature draws upon and feeds back into a larger body of knowledge, is the conventional way in which researchers in the past assumed this responsibility. However, today we need models of synthetic problem formulation for researchers who want instead to generate theories. We, therefore, conclude this chapter with two such models, *paradigmatic pragmatism* and *mixing metaphors,* which take into account both the role of theory and the role of method in defining research problems.

4.4 Paradigmatic Pragmatism

It has become increasingly clear that research methods cannot be assumed a priori to be neutral or a theoretical tool. For example, Walton (1966) demonstrated that the different theories of community power held by political scientists and sociologists might well be a consequence of the fact that researchers in these two disciplines have characteristically studied community power with different types of methods. And Perrucci and Pilisuk (1970) have further shown that the method employed to study community power may not only determine which theory one accepts but may also determine which theories one can formulate and test.

More generally, Ritzer (1980) has posited systematic links between theoretical styles (or paradigms) and research styles (or methods).

Those who accept the social facts paradigm tend to use questionnaires and/or interviews when they do empirical research. Those who accept the social definition paradigm tend to use the observation method in their research. The choice of methods is, of course, made necessary by the nature of the social definition paradigm. All of the methods discussed in this book *could* be used by the social behaviourist...[but]...the behaviourist almost invariably uses the experimental method. However, Platt (1996) in her historical study of sociological methods has cautioned against assuming tight connections between general theoretical orientations and particular types of method. She concludes that "the link between theory and method has been a loose one. It does not follow that it is insignificant, or equally loose in all cases, but it is clear that we need to look elsewhere to explain both the origins of particular methods and the choice of method made in particular projects".

To the extent that theoretical styles and research styles are systematically linked, it may be expected that researchers will pose problems that are compatible with their own particular theoretical orientations and with the methods linked to those orientations, and will ignore problems that are either theoretically or methodologically incompatible. Specific theories and methods may be associated for at least two reasons. First, certain methods may be better suited for gathering data on specific types or classes of variables and these variables may in turn suggest certain types or classes of theoretical concepts and propositions more readily than others. Second, certain theories may contain concepts and propositions that imply types or classes of variables that in turn recommend certain methods as being more appropriate than others. Both of these reasons imply that the form in which research problems are initially posed may be shaped by methodological or theoretical commitments, but neither implies any necessary linkage between or limitation by singular methods and singular theories.

And it is also to be expected that researchers working in different theoretical and methodological styles will frequently disagree about the relative importance of particular research problems and even as to whether particular phenomena or theories are problematic. For example, survey researchers who assume a "common understanding" about questionnaire items are often criticized by phenomenologists (e.g., Cicourel, 1962) who regard such understandings as highly problematic. And human ecologists and demographers who study the relationships between resources and population characteristics are criticized by conflict theorists for ignoring concepts and variables pertaining to political power and governmental structures. Such debates will and should continue until the issues are resolved.

However, the pragmatism of employing multiple research methods to study the same general problem by posing different specific questions has some pragmatic implications for social theory. Rather than being wedded to a particular theoretical style, its pet problems and questions, and its most compatible method, one might instead combine methods that would encourage or even require the integration of different theoretical perspectives to interpret the data. If hypotheses and variables that have been previously isolated each within their own theoretical systems are instead empirically interrelated in the same study, then conceptual linkages between different theoretical systems are more likely to follow.

4.5 Mixing Metaphors to Generate Research Problems

"A stitch in time gathers no moss" may make little sense as a homily, but if one struggled to make sense of it, and then a new meaning or insight might be generated from two common sayings. Mixed metaphors, crossovers of theories, or applications of a theory developed in one subfield to another may provoke new questions, provide useful insights, and suggest new ways of looking at phenomena. Becker's (1963) work on deviance, for example, can be seen as an application of Mead's (1934) concepts and propositions of identity formation in social psychological development to the area of deviance, as can his application of Hughes' (1960) research on work and occupations to the development of concepts and propositions on "deviant careers". "Night as Frontier" (Melbin, 1978), "Neighbourhoods as Fashion," and "Cities as Organisms" are but a few obvious examples of analyses based on the conscious use of metaphorical thinking. Theories of stratification also contain metaphorical concepts related to the physics and chemistry of geology (such as strata, crystallization, and permeable and semi-permeable boundaries).

And the economist Lester Thurow (1996) has borrowed the geological concept of plate tectonics and combined it with the evolutionary biology concept of punctuated equilibrium to explore the future of capitalism: "Today the world is in a state of punctuated equilibrium—which is being caused by the simultaneous movement of five economic plates. In the end a new game with new rules requiring new strategies will emerge. Some of today's players will adapt and learn how to win in the new game. They will be those who understand the movement of the economic tectonic plates. They will become the top-of-the-food-chain, 'fittest' individuals, business firms, or nations. Historically, they will come to be seen as the economic equivalent of mammals".

Early social scientists, of course, also drew heavily on biological or anthropomorphic metaphors—for example, the work of Spencer (1898) and Durkheim (1897/1951). The early Chicago School of Sociology likewise drew heavily upon biological metaphors, especially in its human ecological theories of cities.

The systematic use of metaphorical thinking is closely related to argument by analogy. Analogous thinking requires seeing similarities among disparate entities and asking whether what is known to be true about the one may be generalized to the other. Posing metaphorical questions is not simply a word game, but enters centrally into the social scientist's paradigmatic view of the world, of what is problematic about that world, and of how to conduct empirical research to understand those problems.

According to Kuhn (1970), "puzzle solving" is a characteristic of normal science. Rather than employing explicit rules that define problems and their solutions, scientists work by example, analogy, or metaphor, applying exemplars from one situation to another.

The resultant ability to see a variety of situations as like each other...is, I think, the main thing a student acquires by doing exemplary problems...After he has completed a certain number, which may vary from one individual to the next, he views the situations that confront him as a scientist in the same gestalt as other members of his specialists' group. The legitimacy of the use of exemplars or analogies is ultimately based upon the community of practicing scientists accepting such models. For example, biological analogies have been widely accepted within sociology, whereas models from physics have not. *Social physics* was offered by St. Simon as an alternative label to sociology as a name for the discipline, but only a few analogies from physics are to be found in research. One such is Samuel Stouffer's (1940) *gravity model* (inverse square law) that relates the amount of geographical mobility between cities to the distance between them.

New metaphors and new concepts suggest new variables and new methods—new questions and new data to answer them. As in the parable of the blind men and the elephant, the metaphor used to describe a phenomenon (it is *like a snake* said the man holding the trunk, *like a tree* said the one holding a leg, etc.) depends partially upon the aspect of reality one happens to get hold of. But metaphorical depiction of reality is also determined by the method of observation one uses.

Hearing an elephant, one might liken it to a trumpeter swan; or tasting a juicy, rare elephant steak, one might liken it to a cow. In short, metaphors are often (some say always) used to define reality, and metaphors are in part measurement and method specific. Mixing metaphors can suggest new questions requiring new methods, and mixing methods can generate new questions leading to new metaphors.

4.6 Schools of Thought in Social Research

A science is often thought of as being a coherent body of thought about a topic over which there is a broad consensus among its practitioners. As Alan Chalmers (1999) notes of the popular view of science: When it is claimed that science is special because it is based on the facts, the facts are presumed to be claims about the world that can be directly established by a careful, unprejudiced use of the senses. Science is to be based on what we see, hear and touch rather than on personal opinions or speculative imaginings. If observation of the world is carried out in a careful, unprejudiced way then the facts established in this way will constitute a secure, objective basis for science.

(Chalmers, 1999: 1) Yet the actual practice of science shows that there are not only different perspectives on a given phenomenon, but also alternative methods of gathering information and of analysing the resultant data. While these differences do affect the natural sciences, we are concerned here with the history and practice of the social sciences (see M. Williams, 2000). To have differences of perspective in a site of activity such as social research appears to be problematic. Quite simply, if there is no one established way of working then surely that undermines the idea of a scientific discipline? Perhaps, though, we should challenge the idea that science is an all-embracing explanation of the social or natural world beyond our criticism, or that unity of method is necessarily a good thing. Instead, perhaps these matters are contested in both justification and application because there are political and value considerations which affect our lives? These are not within the power of science to alter, nor in any democracy should they be (see Fuller, 2000). Its role is to understand and explain social phenomena, to focus attention on particular issues and to challenge conventionally held beliefs about the social and natural worlds.

Social research, however, does differ from natural sciences, in that researchers are able to ask questions of those they study: Unlike objects in nature, humans are self-aware beings who confer sense and purposes on what they do. We can't even describe social life accurately unless we first grasp the concepts that people apply in their behaviour (Giddens, 1997: 12-13). We shall also find theories that challenge our understanding of the social world as part of social research practice. In sum, therefore, social sciences are more complicated (and more exciting) than any single definition of their activities could encompass: for example, what constitutes a 'science', the nature of its methods and the types of data which it should collect are open to dispute. In order to see how this arises, it is necessary to describe the main ideas and debates within social science before we move on to examine the relationship between social theory and research.

4.6.1 Objectivity: The Introduction noted that objectivity, along with generalization and explanation, were considered as fundamental characteristics of a science. After all, if we are to hold to the view that social science research offers us knowledge about the social world which is not necessarily available by other means, then we are making some privileged claims about our work. Research thus becomes more than a reflection of our opinions and prejudices: it substantiates, refutes, organizes or generates our theories and produces evidence which may challenge not only our own beliefs, but also those of society in general. It is at this point that the debate over objectivity in the social sciences enters. It is often assumed that if our values do not enter into our research, it is objective and above criticism. Objectivity is therefore defined as the basic conviction that there is or must be some permanent, a historical matrix or framework to which we can ultimately appeal in determining the nature of rationality, knowledge, truth, reality, goodness, or rightness (Bernstein, 1983: 8).

Many people accept what scientists say is the 'truth'. On the other hand, the subject matter of the social sciences is social life itself. People are obviously fundamental to social life and the question is now raised that as social researchers and as members of a society, is it possible or desirable for us to suspend our sense of belonging? Different perspectives have provided answers to this question.

4.6.2 Positivism: We may argue that people react to their environment much as molecules which become 'excited' when heat is applied to a liquid. Clearly, science does not have then to ask the molecules what they think. So is it necessary that we, as social scientists, ask people? We may, of course, be interested in people's opinions in terms of their reactions to events that affect their lives, but only in so far as they are reacting and we wish to explain and predict their behaviour accordingly. However, don't we all believe that we possess something called free-will? That is we can, to some extent, control our own destinies rather than have it controlled, like the molecules, by a change in our environment. In other words, that we can 'act on', as well as behave in 'reaction to', our social environments. Some experiments in the natural sciences take the form of altering the environment and seeing how people react to it.

The problem here is one of controlling the inputs into experimental situations in order to see what changes cause particular alterations in behaviour. There are problems with this approach, hence the idea of 'quasi-experimentation' as an approximation towards this model of research. In some approaches to evaluation research, for example, a group is selected who will be subject to the programme which is to be evaluated. This treatment group will then be compared to those who have not been subject to the programme. Nevertheless, we must ask: is social life really like that? Are experiments in a laboratory artificial and so do not reflect the complications, decisions and contradictions involved in social life?

If we believe ourselves to be the product of our environment—created by it—then to some extent we are the mirror image of it. It defines our nature, or our being. We do not have to ask the people themselves because we can predict how they will behave through reference to environmental factors alone. Simply expressed, this is the position of two schools of thought in social research: behaviourism and positivism. However, it should be noted that positivism refers to varied traditions of social and philosophical thought and given that the term is often used in a pejorative sense without due regard to its history, it runs the risk of being devoid of any specific meaning (Bryant, 1985).

For one author inclined toward positivism, the social scientist must study social phenomena 'in the same state of mind as the physicist, chemist or physiologist when he probes into a still unexplored region of the scientific domain' (Durkheim, 1964: xiv). Objectivity is then defined by being the same as that of natural science and social life may be explained in the same way as natural phenomena. This tradition may therefore be characterized in terms of the prediction and explanation of the behaviour of phenomena and the pursuit of objectivity, which is defined as the researcher's 'detachment' from the topic under investigation.

The results of research using this method of investigation are then said to produce a set of 'true', precise and wide-ranging 'laws' (known as covering laws) of human behaviour. We would then be able to generalize from our observations on social phenomena to make statements about the behaviour of the population as a whole. Positivism thus explains human behaviour in terms of cause and effect (in our example above, heat is the cause and the effect is the molecules becoming excited as the temperature increases) and 'data' must then be collected on the social environment and people's reactions to it.

4.6.3 Empiricism: If the aim of positivism is to collect and assemble data on the social world from which we can generalize and explain human behaviour through the use of our theories, then it shares with empiricism the belief that there are 'facts' which we can gather on the social world, *independently* of how people interpret them. As researchers, we simply need to refine our instruments of data collection in order that they are neutral recording instruments much as the ruler measures distance and the clock, time. The fundamental difference between empiricism and positivism, however, lies in the realm of theory. Data within positivism is theory-driven and designed to test the accuracy of the theory. Empiricism, on the other hand, is a method of research which has not referred explicitly to the theory guiding its data collection procedures. It is thus characterized 'by the catchphrase "the facts speak for themselves" (Bulmer, 1982b: 31).

It is important, as happens all too often, not to confuse the words empirical and empiricism. The word empirical refers to the collection of data on the social world to test, generate or interact with the propositions of social science, while, as Martin Bulmer's quote indicates, the empiricist school of thought believes that the facts speak for themselves and require no explanation via theoretical engagement. While there are differences between positivism and empiricism, the former does rely on the methods of the latter. They also both assert that there are facts about the social world which we can gather—*independent of* variations due to interpretation. Objectivity is then defined in terms of researchers' detachment from the social world, as well as the accuracy of their data collection instruments. Quite simply, there is a world out there that we can record and we can analyze independently of people's interpretations of it. This follows the 'correspondence theory of reality' which holds that a belief, statement or sentence is true as long as there is an external fact that corresponds to it.

4.6.4 Realism: Realism shares with positivism the aim of explanation. Beyond that similarity the parallels end. A branch of realism, known as 'critical realism' (the two are frequently, and wrongly, conflated), has enjoyed a particular boost in the social sciences with the works of Roy Bhaskar (Archer *et al.*, 1998) who states: Normally to be a realist in philosophy is to be committed to the existence of some disputed kind of being (e.g. material objects, universals, causal laws; propositions, numbers, probabilities; efficacious reasons, social structures, moral facts). (Bhaskar, 1993: 308) Realism has a long history and may be associated with the works of Karl Marx and Sigmund Freud (see M. Williams and May, 1996: 81-88). Marx, for example, constructed his typology (a method of classification) of capitalism on the basis that there are certain essential features which distinguish it from other economic and political systems. Within this economic system there exist 'central structural mechanisms' and the task of researchers is 'to organize one's concepts so as to grasp *its* essential features successfully' (Keat and Urry, 1975: 112, original emphasis).

In referring to underlying structural mechanisms, an important argument within this perspective is being employed. If researchers simply content .themselves with studying everyday social life, such as conversations and interactions between people, this will distract them from an investigation of the underlying mechanisms which make those possible in the first instance (Collier, 1994; Sayer, 2000). The task of researchers within this tradition is to uncover the structures of social relations in order to understand why we then have the policies and practices that we do. Similarly, Sigmund Freud argued that our consciousness was determined by our sub-consciousness. Thus, people's neuroses are the visible manifestations of their sexual and aggressive desires that are repressed in their subconscious. Freud's single contribution to social thought may thus be said to lie 'in the idea that culture is reproduced through a repressive structuring of unconscious passions' (Elliott, 1994: 41). While people may not be directly aware of the causes of these experiences, they still affect their actions.

Realism argues that the knowledge people have of their social world affects their behaviour and, unlike the propositions of positivism and empiricism, the social world does not simply 'exist' independently of this knowledge. Given this, causes are not simply determining of actions, but must be seen as 'tendencies' that produce particular effects. Yet people's knowledge may be partial or incomplete. The task of social research, therefore, is not simply to collect observations on the social world, but to explain these within theoretical frameworks which examine the underlying mechanisms which inform people's actions and prevent their choices from reaching fruition: for example, how schools function to reproduce a workforce for capitalism despite the resistance that may take place in the classroom (P. Willis, 1977). As Bob Carter puts it in his examination of the relationship between realism and racism: 'realism is resolutely post-empiricist in its stress on the theory-driven nature of social scientific knowledge' (Carter, 2000: 171).

The aim of examining and explaining underlying mechanisms cannot use the methods of empiricism as these simply reflect the everyday world, not the conditions which make it possible. Therefore, along with others in this tradition (Sayer, 1992), Keat and Urry (1975) argue that realism must utilize a different definition of science to positivism. In particular, a realist conception of social science would not necessarily assume that we can 'know' the world out there independently of the ways in which we describe it. That is not to say, however, that social reality is not stratified: for example, into individual, interactive and institutional levels. Access to these different layers of reality is the task of a realist research programme and bringing to the attention of people—how they affect their actions in a situation of dialogue and cooperation.

It is this philosophy, in contrast to other approaches to evaluation (see Clarke with Dawson, 1999), that underlies Ray Pawson and Nick Tilley's (1997) recommendations for the conduct of programme evaluation. Furthermore, as Dave Byrne puts it in his exposition of complexity theory, it too shares with critical realism an 'insistence on the emergent material character of understanding in particular and social action in general' (Byrne, 1998: 51). Given the above, there are those within this tradition who have built bridges between the idea that there is a world out there independent of our interpretation of it (empiricism and positivism) and the need for researchers to understand the process by which people interpret the world. Before discussing those who have attempted this, we shall first examine the perspectives which argue, contrary to positivism and empiricism, that there is no social world 'beyond' people's perceptions and interpretations.

4.6.5 Subjectivity: Up to now, we have spoken of the ways in which our environment or its underlying structures—of which we are not necessarily aware—structure us, or create us as objects (positivism) or subjects and objects (realism). Perhaps you are not happy with the idea that you are created or formed in this way. We like to believe that we exercise free-will and make judgments which alter the courses of our lives. Positivism does not pay much attention to the detail of people's inner mental states.

Realism, on the other hand, may refer to people's consciousness in so far as it reflects the conditions under which they live, how structures are reproduced and their desires and needs are frustrated. When we refer to people's consciousness we are concerned with what takes place—in terms of thinking and acting—within each of us. These subjective states refer to our 'inner' world of experiences, rather than the world 'out there'. To concentrate on subjectivity we focus on the *meanings* that people give to their environment, not the environment itself. Contrary to the contentions of positivists we, as researchers, cannot know this independently of people's interpretations of it. The only thing that we can know with certainty is how people interpret the world around them. Our central interest, as researchers, is now focused upon people's understandings and interpretations of their social environments, part of which has been termed a 'phenomenological' approach to researching the social world (see Moustakas, 1994).

4.6.6 Idealism: Some schools of thought emphasize our creation of the social world through the realm of ideas, rather than our being simply conditioned or created by it. They would argue that our actions are not governed by cause and effect, as in the case of molecules in a test tube, but by the rules which we use to interpret the world. As natural science deals with matter which is not 'conscious', researchers of this persuasion argue that its methods cannot deal with social life and should therefore be discarded from its study. To speak of cause and effect is not applicable to researching social life for people contemplate, interpret and act within their environments. For these reasons, the methods of the social sciences are fundamentally different from, but *not* inferior to, the natural sciences.

It is the world of ideas in which we are interested as social researchers: 'Such a viewpoint suggests that human activity is not behaviour (an adaption to material conditions), but an expression of meaning that humans give (via language) to their conduct' (Johnson *et al.*, 1990: 14). Rules exist in social action through which we produce society and understand and recognize each other. Rules, of course, are often broken and also subject to different interpretations. For that reason, we cannot predict human behaviour but people still act as if they were following rules and this makes their actions intelligible. People are constantly engaged in the process of interpretation and it is this which we should seek to understand. In other words, researchers should concentrate upon *how* people produce social life.

Social life can be understood only through an examination of people's selection and interpretation of events and actions. Understanding these processes and the rules which make them possible is the aim of research for schools of thought within this tradition. It is not explaining why people behave in certain ways by reference to their subconscious states or environmental conditions, but how people interpret the world and interact with each other. This process is known as *inter-subjectivity*.

The idea of an external social 'reality' has now been abandoned because the meanings which we attach to the world are not static, nor universal, but always multiple and variable and constantly subject to modification and change. Our accounts of the social world must therefore be 'internalist': that is, arising from within the cultures we are studying. As one advocate of this view puts it in relation to meaning and language use: 'To give an account of the meaning of a word is to describe how it is used; and to describe how it is used is to describe the social intercourse into which it enters' (Winch, 1990: 123). There are those within this tradition who argue that researchers need to employ 'hermeneutic principles'; hermeneutics referring to the theory and practice of interpretation.

We are no longer proclaiming our 'disengagement' from our subject matter as a condition of science (positivism), but our 'commitment' and 'engagement' as a condition of understanding social life. Our sense of belonging to a society and the techniques which we use for understanding are not impediments to our studies.

The procedures through which we understand and interpret our social world are now necessary conditions for us to undertake research. In the process we both utilize and challenge our understandings in doing social science research and the social researcher stands at the centre of the research process as a requirement of interpreting social life. The idea of science is now very different from positivism and empiricism. For these reasons, there is a tendency in this tradition of social thought to prefer methods of research such as participant observation and focused interviewing.

4.6.7 Building Bridges: There are those who have attempted to synthesize some aspects of these major perspectives. One social theorist, in particular, has argued that our everyday actions are meaningful to us, but they also reproduce structures which both enable and constrain our actions (Giddens, 1976, 1984, 1996), a position shared by Roy Bhaskar, whose work was noted earlier. Pierre Bourdieu is also a thinker whose work has been driven by empirical interests and so has developed a series of 'tools' for researching and thinking about the social world (for example, see Bourdieu and Wacquant, 1992; Bourdieu, 1993; Bourdieu with Saint Martin, 1995; Bourdieu *et al.*, 1999).

The insights of psychoanalysis and linguistics have also been employed to argue that while human actions are meaningful and variable; this does not mean that we cannot then agree on what is valid or 'true' about the social world. This bridge-building attempt fuses the twin aims of 'how' (understanding) and 'why' (explanation) in social research (Habermas, 1984, 1987, 1989, 1990).

There is also the school of 'post-structuralism', which includes the French philosopher Jacques Derrida, as well as Michel Foucault until his death in 1984. Foucault's thought, in particular, evolved in reaction to both the subjectivism of some social science perspectives and the naive empiricism imported from the natural sciences (Foucault, 1977; 1980). His work is thus characterized as moving beyond structuralism and hermeneutics, towards an 'interpretive analytics' (Dreyfus and Rabinow, 1982). In the process, Foucault considers knowledge and power to be constructed within a set of social practices. The result is to question the concept of truth as separable from the exercise of power. As interesting and provocative as these ideas are, they have often been discussed at a socio-theoretical and philosophical level.

Yet, Foucault himself was a careful social researcher and while he used his research sources in different ways, it is possible to interpret his work for the purposes of doing social research and to draw parallels with the actor network theory of Michel Callon and Bruno Latour (see Kendall and Wickham,

1999; Law and Hassard, 1999). While an exposition of these ideas and their implications for research are well beyond the stated aims of this book, I have deliberately included them so you can refer directly to their works, or studies about their works (see Morrow with Brown, 1994; May, 1996; M. Dean, 1999). They demonstrate the ingenuity with which social thinkers have attempted to tackle issues which are so central to social research.

4.6.8 Post-modernism: Before moving on to the section on feminist research, we need to consider a perspective about which there is much discussion, but often little clarification. As we shall see later on, post-modernism shares with feminist relativism the belief that knowledge is both local and contingent and there are no standards beyond particular contexts through which we may judge its truth or falsity. Although there are those who are labelled as post-modernists who exhibit clear differences in their perspectives, post-modernism refers to a cultural perspective or movement and/or epistemology, while post-modernization relates to a process that is said to lead to the historical epoch known as post-modernity (Lyon, 1999; Delanty, 2000).

Therefore, it is important to note that one does not necessarily have to become a post-modernist in order to accept some of its insights regarding the changing times through which we are living. Indeed, 'post-modernism' is often used as a convenient label around which to base a series of observations on contemporary issues (Bauman, 1997). Post-modernists are anti-foundationalists.

Whether talking about implosions of meaning with the consequence that the world becomes devoid of any meaning (Baudrillard, 1983a), or of the computer age and the severing of the link between knowledge and legitimacy or of the potential for dialogue within a liberal consensus in which scientific claims to truth about the social and natural worlds have little place (Rorty, 1989), post-modernists exhibit the same underlying tendency: that is, that there are no universal standards against which science may lay claim in order to validate its standards.

Quite simply, objectivity gives way to relativism with the result that not only science, but also truth, goodness, justice, rationality, and so on, are concepts relative to time and place: 'Since every act of cognition necessarily occurs within a particular perspective, relativism claims that no rational basis exists for judging one perspective better than any other' (Fay, 1996: 2). What have been termed the 'repressed rivals' of science—religion, folk knowledge, narrative and myth—are now said to be returning to 'take their revenge' (Seidman, 1998). It is significant that it is within the humanities and the area of cultural studies that these views have found their greatest legitimacy.

Yet how this translates into a practical research programme, without contradiction and retaining the relevance of research, is a matter of some considerable difficulty, let alone dispute. Take, for example, the idea of truth which underlies research. Must not all communities, including those conducting research, assume a truth which lies beyond that which they propagate in order to legitimize their beliefs and practices in the first instance? If so, relativism must pre-suppose the existence of something beyond itself.

In considering all of the above perspectives, the waters are far muddier than suggested. For instance, Durkheim is often termed a positivist but would not simply deny the place of subjectivity in social life, nor would an idealist necessarily deny objectivity defined as 'detachment' from the social world, while Foucault in discussing the implications of his work noted that if these meant 'one is a positivist, then, I am happy to be one' (Foucault, 1972: 125). However, there remain differences; in particular whether the social science are the same or different from the natural science and whether human actions, unlike the observed effects of phenomena in the physical world, are meaningful and intentional.

5

Variables in Social Science Research

A *variable* is something that can change, such as 'gender' and are typically the focus of a study.

Attributes are sub-values of a variable, such as 'male' and 'female'. An *exhaustive* list contains all possible answers, for example gender could also include 'male transgender' and 'female transgender' (and both can be pre- or post-operative).

Mutually exclusive attributes are those that cannot occur at the same time. Thus, in a survey a person may be requested to select one answer from a list of alternatives (as opposed to selecting as many that might apply).

Quantitative data is numeric. This is useful for mathematical and statistical analysis that leads to a predictive formula.

Qualitative data is based on human judgment. You can turn qualitative data into quantitative data, for example by counting the proportion of people who hold a particular qualitative viewpoint.

Units are the ways that variables are classified. These include: individuals, groups, social interactions and objects.

5.1 Types of Variables

1. *Descriptive variables* are those that which will be reported on, without relating them to anything in particular.
2. *Categorical variables* result from a selection from categories, such as 'agree' and 'disagree'. Nominal and ordinal variables are categorical.
3. *Numeric variables* give a number, such as age.
4. *Discrete variables* are numeric variables that come from a limited set of numbers. They may result from, answering questions such as 'how many', 'how often', etc.

5. *Continuous variables* are numeric variables that can take any value, such as weight.

5.1.1 Nature of Dependency: Variables are classified on the basis of nature of dependency.

1. An *independent variable* is one is manipulated by the researcher. It is like the knob on a dial that the researcher turns. In graphs, it is put on the X-axis.
2. A *dependent variable* is one which changes as a result of the independent variable being changed, and is put on the Y-axis in graphs.

The Holy Grail for researchers is to be able to determine the relationship between the independent and dependent variables, such that if the independent variable is changed, then the researcher will be able to accurately predict how the dependent variable will change.

Extraneous variables are additional variables which could provide alternative explanations or cast doubt on conclusions. Variables may have the following characteristics:

1. **Period:** When it starts and stops.
2. **Pattern:** Daily, weekly, ad-hoc etc.
3. **Detail:** Overview through to 'in-depth'.
4. **Latency:** Time between measuring dependent and independent variable (some things take time to take effect).

Note that in an experiment there may be many additional variables beyond the manipulated independent variable and the measured dependent variables. It is critical in experiments that these variables do not vary and hence bias or otherwise distort the results. There is a struggle between control vs. authenticity in managing this.

5.2 Correlation

With perfect correlation, the X-Y graph of points (as a scatter diagram) will give a straight line. Whilst this may happen in physics, it seldom happens in social research and a probabilistic relationship is the best that can be determined.

Correlation can be positive (increasing X increases Y), negative (increasing X decreases Y) or non-linear (increasing X makes Y increase or decrease, depending on the value of X). Correlation can also be partial, that is across only a range of values X. As all possible values of X can seldom be tested, most correlations found are at best partial.

When correlation is determined, a further question is whether varying the independent variable *caused* the independent variable to change. This adds complexity and debate to the situation.

Sometimes a third variable is the cause, such as when a correlation between ice-cream sales and drowning is actually due to the fact that both are caused by warm weather.

5.3 Continuous (or Quantitative) Variables and Discrete (or Qualitative) Variables

We can distinguish between two types of variables according to the level of measurement:

1. Continuous or quantitative variables.
2. Discrete or qualitative variables.

A quantitative variable is one in which the variants differ in magnitude, e.g., income, age, GNP etc. A qualitative variable is one in which the variants differ in kind rather than in magnitude, e.g., marital status, gender, nationality etc.

5.3.1 Continuous or Quantitative Variables: Continuous variables can be classified into three categories:

A. Interval-scale Variables: Interval scale data has order and equal intervals. Interval scale variables are measured on a linear scale, and can take on positive or negative values. It is assumed that the intervals keep the same importance throughout the scale. They allow us not only to rank order the items that are measured but also to quantify and compare the magnitudes of differences between them. We can say that the temperature of 40°C is higher than 30°C, and an increase from 20°C to 40°C is twice as much as the increase from 30°C to 40°C. Counts are interval scale measurements, such as counts of publications or citations, years of education, etc.

B. Continuous Ordinal Variables: They occur when the measurements are continuous, but one is not certain whether they are on a linear scale, the only trustworthy information being the rank order of the observations. For example, if a scale is transformed by an exponential, logarithmic or any other nonlinear monotonic transformation, it loses its interval - scale property. Here, it would be expedient to replace the observations by their ranks.

C. Ratio-scale Variables: These are continuous positive measurements on a nonlinear scale. A typical example is the growth of bacterial population (say, with a growth function Ae^{Bt}). In this model, equal time intervals multiply the population by the same ratio. Hence, the name ratio-scale.

Ratio data are also interval data, but they are not measured on a linear scale. With interval data, one can perform logical operations, add, and subtract, but one cannot multiply or divide. For instance, if a liquid is at 40 degrees and we add 10 degrees, it will be 50 degrees. However, a liquid at 40 degrees does not have twice the temperature of a liquid at 20 degrees because 0 degrees does not represent "no temperature"—to multiply or divide in this way we would have to use the Kelvin temperature scale, with a true zero point (0 degrees Kelvin = -273.15 degrees Celsius). In social sciences, the issue of "true zero" rarely arises, but one should be aware of the statistical issues involved.

There are three different ways to handle the ratio-scaled variables.

1. Simply as interval scale variables. However, this procedure should be avoided as it can distort the results.
2. As continuous ordinal scale.
3. By transforming the data (for example, logarithmic transformation) and then treating the results as interval scale variables.

5.3.2 Qualitative or Discrete Variables: Discrete variables are also called categorical variables. A discrete variable 'X' can take on a finite number of numerical values, categories or codes. Discrete variables can be classified into the following categories:

1. Nominal variables.
2. Ordinal variables.
3. Dummy variables from quantitative variables.
4. Preference variables.
5. Multiple response variables.

A. Nominal Variables: Nominal variables allow for only qualitative classification. That is, they can be measured only in terms of whether the individual items belong to certain distinct categories, but we cannot quantify or even rank order the categories: Nominal data has no order, and the assignment of numbers to categories is purely arbitrary. Because of lack of order or equal intervals, one cannot perform arithmetic (+, -, /, *) or logical operations (>, <, =) on the nominal data.

Table 5.1: An illustration of Nominal Variables

Gender	1. Male 2. Female
Marital Status	1. Unmarried 2. Married 3. Divorcee 4. Widower

B. Ordinal Variables: A discrete ordinal variable is a nominal variable, but its different states are ordered in a meaningful sequence. Ordinal data has order, but the intervals between scale points may be uneven. Because of lack of equal distances, arithmetic operations are impossible, but logical operations can be performed on the ordinal data. A typical example of an ordinal variable is the socio-economic status of families. We know 'upper middle' is higher than 'middle' but we cannot say 'how much higher'. Ordinal variables are quite useful for subjective assessment of 'quality; importance or relevance'. Ordinal scale data are very frequently used in social and behavioural research. Almost all opinion surveys today request answers on three-, five-, or seven-point scales. Such data are not appropriate for analysis by classical techniques, because the numbers are comparable only in terms of relative magnitude, not actual magnitude.

Consider for example, a questionnaire item on the time involvement of scientists in the 'perception and identification of research problems'. The respondents were asked to indicate their involvement by selecting one of the following codes:
1 = Very low or nil.
2 = Low.
3 = Medium.
4 = Great.
5 = Very great.

Here, the variable 'time involvement' is an ordinal variable with 5 states.

Ordinal variables often cause confusion in data analysis. Some statisticians treat them as nominal variables. Other statisticians treat them as interval scale variables, assuming that the underlying scale is continuous, but because of the lack of a sophisticated instrument, they could not be measured on an interval scale.

C. Dummy Variables from Quantitative Variables: A quantitative variable can be transformed into a categorical variable, called a dummy variable by recoding the values.

Table 5.2: Dummy Variables from Quantitative Variables

[Up to 25]	1
[25, 40]	2
[40, 50]	3
[50, 60]	4
[Above 60]	5

Consider the following example: the quantitative variable *Age* can be classified into five intervals. The values of the associated categorical variable, called dummy variables, are 1, 2, 3, 4, and 5.

D. Preference Variables: Preference variables are specific discrete variables, whose values are either in a decreasing or increasing order. For example, in a survey, a respondent may be asked to indicate the importance of the following nine sources of information in his research and development work, by using the code [1] for the most important source and [9] for the least important source:

1. Literature published in the country.
2. Literature published abroad.
3. Scientific abstracts.
4. Unpublished reports, material etc.
5. Discussions with colleagues within the research unit.
6. Discussions with colleagues outside the research unit but within institution.
7. Discussions with colleagues outside the institution.

It may be noted that preference data is also ordinal. The interval distance from the first preference to the second preference is not the same as, for example, from the sixth to the seventh preference.

E. Multiple Response Variables: Multiple response variables are those, which can assume more than one value. A typical example is a survey questionnaire about the use of computers in research. The respondents were asked to indicate the purpose(s) for which they use computers in their research work. The respondents could score more than one category.

1. Statistical analysis.
2. Lab automation/ process control.
3. Data base management, storage and retrieval.
4. Modelling and simulation.
5. Scientific and engineering calculations.
6. Computer aided design (CAD).
7. Communication and networking.
8. Graphics.

6

Sampling in Research

6.1 Meaning and Definition

For studying a social problem, it is difficult to study whole universe of the problem under study. In such a case, sampling has become commonplace idea. A sampling is a small proportion of a population selected for observation and analysis. It is a collection of items or elements from a population. By observing the characteristics of sample, one can make certain inference about the characteristics of the population from it is drawn; the act so involved is called sampling. Sampling can be defined as the selection of some part of an aggregate or totality, the bases of which a judgment or inference about the aggregate or totality is made. It is the process of obtaining information about an entire population by examining a part of it.

According to F.N. Kerlinger, "Sampling is taking any portion of a population or universe as representative of the population." According to Y.D. Keskar, "Sampling is the generalization in terms of the whole group through the facts assembled relate to only part of it".

Virtually every research study uses sampling method of some kind to generalize about population. It is deliberate rather than haphazard.

6.2 Essentials of Sampling

1. **Representativeness:** A sample should be selected in such a manner that it really represents the universe.
2. **Adequacy:** The size of the sample selected should be adequate and sufficient to represent the population.
3. **Independence:** All items of the population should have the same chance of being selected in the sample.

4. **Homogeneity:** There should be no basic difference in the nature of units of the universe and that of the same.
5. **Accuracy:** An accurate sample is one which exactly represents the population.

6.3 Technical Terms in Sampling

The terms and procedures that are outlined as follows are appropriate for sampling anything, including social groups, census blocks, or any other objects that are needed in a sample.

1. **Element:** According to Bailey, the objects of study are called the units of analysis. These units are also called as sampling elements, a term that refers to the elements or units about which information will be gathered. The sampling elements for sociologists are almost always the individual human being, but they can also be groups, clubs, and formal organizations, or almost any "thing" that we are interested in studying.
2. **Population:** The sum total of the elements is called the population or universe. It is the aggregate of all elements defined prior to the selection of sample. Population can be finite or infinite.
3. **Sampling Unit:** A sampling unit is either a single sampling element or an aggregation of elements. It is the element available for selection at some stage of the sampling process, for example female 18-50 years. In a simple random sampling, the sample units are generally the individual cases that comprise the sample. However, in a multi-stage sample, the first stage, called the primary sampling units, are aggregates or clusters of cases such as geographic areas or specified groups from within which the final sampling units are selected.
4. **Sampling Frame:** A sampling frame is a complete list of all sampling units available for selection from the population.
5. **Sample Size:** A sample size states how many to be surveyed. For example: should 50 or 60 students be interviewed?

6.4 Characteristics of Good Sampling

1. A sample should be representative of the whole population.
2. A sample should be independent i.e. inter-changeability of units. Each unit should be free to include in the sample.
3. The size of the sample should be adequate to generalize.
4. Conclusions to the whole population.
5. A sample should be free from prejudice and bias.
6. A sample should be in coeternity with the objective of the study.
7. The units included in the sample should be homogenous.
8. Sampling should result in small sampling error.
9. Sampling should be economy in terms of time, cost and effort.
10. Sampling should have scientific base.

6.5 Sample Design

A sample design is a definite plan for obtaining a sample from a given population. It refers to the procedure the researcher will adopt in selecting items from the sample. It is designed before data collection. In designing a sample, the researcher must consider three things: sampling frame, selection of sampling items and sample size. The basic components of a sample design are:

1. Choosing the sample units (who are to be surveyed).
2. Choosing the sample size (how many to be surveyed).
3. Choosing the sample procedure (how to ensure that those who are to be interviewed are included in the sample).
4. Choosing the media (how to reach respondents in the sample-through mail survey, personal interview, telephone interview).

6.6 Types of Sampling Methods

Sampling is broadly divided into two, Probability and Non-Probability techniques as follows:

1. Probability sampling.
2. Non-probability sampling.

6.6.1 Probability Sampling: In it, each item or element in universe has equal chance of being selected. It is called random/chance sampling. Each element of the population has known chance of being selected for the sample. The sampling is done by mathematical decision rules that leave no discretion to the researcher or field interviewer. Four main types of probability sampling are:

A. Simple Random Sampling: In it, the individual observation or individuals are chosen in such a way that each has chance of being selected, and each choice is independent of any other choice. This is used only in those studies where entire population can be listed that are finite population.

Example: If we wished to draw a sample of 50 individuals from a population of 600 students in a college, we can use simple random sampling.

B. Systematic Random Sampling or Systematic Sampling: It consists of the selection of each nth term from a list. First, the item is randomly selected and then a sample item at every nth interval is selected. It is simplest and widely used method of drawing sample. It is used when population size is large and when it become very tiresome to use table of random number to select a sample.

C. Stratified Random Sampling or Stratified Sampling: It involves dividing the population in strata (sub-group). It is used when we have to select sample from a heterogeneous population. Example: If a researcher has to select 300 students from a college for study, he has to first stratify the student population into two strata; their sex—male and female or in a similar way.

D. Cluster or Area or Multistage Sampling: It is a success random of sampling of units or sets and subsets. Cluster is naturally occurring group of participants. They are randomly selected. Once the cluster has been selected, then all participants within the cluster are surveyed. It is also called multistage sampling because sample selection passes through a sequence of stage. Example: District of the country can be randomly selected, then schools, then classes and finally pupils.

6.6.2 Non-probability Sampling: In it, all items in the population don't have equal chance of being selected, it uses that ever subjects are available rather than following a specific subject selection process. Samples are determined by personnel convenience or judgment of the researcher but not by chance. The various type of non probability sampling is as follows.

A. Convenience Sampling*:* It refers to samples selection on the basis of convenience of the researcher. A sample is chosen purely for expedience because it is cheap to find. The sample then would not necessarily be a representative one. Commonly used convenient samples are friends, relatives, family members, associations etc.

B. Purposive/Judgment Sampling*:* It refers to the sample selected on the basis of what some experts think particular sampling units or elements will contribute to answering particular questions at hand. It is an expert .judgment based sampling. Using this method, specialists in the subject matter of the survey choose what they believe to be the best sample for that particular study. It is moderately used in practice. Example: A group of sales manager might select sample of grocery stores in city that they regard as representative in some sense.

C. Quota Sampling: Quota sampling derives its name from the practice assigning quotes or proportions of kind of people to interviewers. It involves three steps; Selection of control characteristics (sex, age, education, etc.) and determination of the proportion of the universe having equal set of characteristics. Allocation of the sample among cells (how large a sample should be taken from each cell) Selection of the sample item. Example: An interviewer may be instructed to conduct the interviews with people 30 years old and half with people under 30 years. Here, the control characteristic is the age of respondents.

D. Sequential Sampling: In fixed-size sampling, the number of items is decided upon in advance whereas in sequential sampling, the number of items is not presented. Studies can be done on only a single unit or the population or a group of population units at a time. The measurement or each group is cumulated with those of previously measured groups. The data are analyzed as they are assembled and sample size is not predetermined. The mathematics underlying sequential samplings are more complex and time consuming.

E. Snowball Sampling: It refers to a procedure in which initial respondents are selected randomly but where additional respondents are then obtained from referral or by other information provided by the initial respondents. One uses this method where respondents are difficult to identify and are best located through referral network. The "snowball" gather subjects as it rolls along. It is widely used to study drug culture, teenage gang activities, community relations etc. Its purpose is to estimate various characteristics that are rare in the total population.

6.7 Sampling in Quantitative Research

The sampling methods used in a quantitative research are as under:

1. Random Sampling Techniques
- Simple random sampling
- Systematic sampling
- Stratified random sampling
➢ proportional
➢ disproportional
- Cluster random sampling
➢ One-stage
➢ Two-stage
2. Non-random Sampling Techniques
- Convenience sampling
- Quota sampling
- Purposive sampling

- Snowball sampling

6.8 Sampling in Qualitative Research

Even if it were possible, it is not necessary to collect data from everyone in a community in order to get valid findings. In qualitative research, only a sample (that is, a subset) of a population is selected for any given study. The study's research objectives and the characteristics of the study population (such as size and diversity) determine which and how many people to select.

In this section, we briefly describe three of the most common sampling methods used in qualitative research: purposive sampling, quota sampling, and snowball sampling. As data collectors, you will not be responsible for selecting the sampling method. The explanations below are meant to help you understand the reasons for using each method.

6.8.1 Purposive Sampling: Purposive sampling, one of the most common sampling strategies, groups participants according to pre-selected criteria relevant to a particular research question (for example, HIV-positive women in capital city). Sample sizes, which may or may not be fixed prior to data collection, depend on the resources and time available, as well as the study's objectives. Purposive sample sizes are often determined on the basis of theoretical saturation (the point in data collection when new data no longer bring additional insights to the research questions). Purposive sampling is therefore most successful when data review and analysis are done in conjunction with data collection.

6.8.2 Quota Sampling: Quota sampling, sometimes considered a type of purposive sampling, is also common. In quota sampling, we decide while designing the study how many people with which characteristics to include as participants. Characteristics might include age, place of residence, gender, class, profession, marital status, use of a particular contraceptive method, HIV status, etc. The criteria we choose allow us to focus on people we think would be most likely to experience, know about, or have insights into the research topic. Then we go into the community and—using recruitment strategies appropriate to the location, culture, and study population—find people who fit these criteria, until we meet the prescribed quotas.

6.8.3 Difference between Purposive and Quota Sampling: Purposive and quota sampling are similar in that they both seek to identify participants based on selected criteria. However, quota sampling is more specific with respect to sizes and proportions of sub-samples, with subgroups chosen to reflect corresponding proportions in the population. If, for example, gender is a variable of interest in how people experience HIV infection, a quota sample would seek an equal balance of HIV-positive men and HIV-positive women in a given city, assuming a 1:1 gender ratio in the population. Studies employ purposive rather than quota sampling when the number of participants is more of a target than a steadfast requirement – that is, an approximate rather than a strict quota.

6.8.4 Snowball Sampling: A third type of sampling, snowballing—also known as chain referral sampling—is considered a type of purposive sampling. In this method, participants or informants with whom contact has already been made use their social networks to refer the researcher to other people who could potentially participate in or contribute to the study. Snowball sampling is often used to find and recruit "hidden populations", that is, groups not easily accessible to researchers through other sampling strategies.

7

Hypotheses and Levels of Measurement

7.1 Hypotheses in Social Sciences

The word hypothesis is a compound of two words 'hypo' and 'thesis' where 'hypo' means under and 'thesis' means reason or rational view. Thus, hypothesis is a below reasoned view. It is a view, which is not fully reasoned. In social research and other research, hypothesis is used to mean a statement about the relationship, which helps to be investigated.

According to F.N. Kerlinger, "Hypothesis is the most powerful tool man has invented to achieve dependable knowledge". Once the problem to be answer is defined, the researcher formulates theory. Theory formulation leads to hypothesis formulation.

Data collection and analysis revolve around the hypothesis, when hypothesis comes to be true, it originates theory. Hypothesis is an educated guess about a problem's solution. It shows the relation between two or more variables, which need to be investigated for the truth. Non-hypothesis can be defined as logically conjectured relationship between two or more variables in testable statements. Hypothesis is always presented in declarative sentence form. They can be general or specific.

According to G.A. Lundberg, "A hypothesis is a tentative generalization the validity of which remains to be tested. It may be any hunch, imaginative idea or intuition whatsoever, which becomes the basis of action or investigation".

According to W. Goode and P.K. Hatt, "A hypothesis is a proposition, which can be put to test to determine its validity. It may seem contrary to, or in accordance with common sense".

Examples of Hypothesis: Family planning can reduce the

growth of population. There is no relationship between working condition and job satisfaction of workers.

7.1.1 Types of Research Hypothesis: These are as under:

A. Null Hypothesis: Null hypothesis is one, which indicates a definitive exact relationship between two variables. It is so called because this hypothesis usually reflect 'no difference' or 'no effect' situation. It means that there is no difference between two populations in aspect of some property and that the difference if any is only accidental and unimportant. The null hypothesis is akin to the principle that a man is innocent until he is proved guilty. It constitutes a challenge and the function of a research to give facts a chance to reflect this challenge. Example:

There is no difference between male and female in their productivity.

Statistically expressed: Ho: $\mu 1 = \mu 2$

Where, Ho is null hypothesis

$\mu 1$ is the productivity of male worker.

$\mu 2$ is the productivity of female worker.

B. Alternative Hypothesis: It is opposite of the null hypothesis. The alternative hypothesis is a statement, which expresses a relationship between two variables or indicates difference between groups. It is the statement of acceptance condition for each of the alternative courses of action or solution to problem. Example: male worker will have more productivity than female workers.

Statistically expressed: $H1 = \mu 1 > \mu 2$

Where H1= alternative hypothesis

$\mu 1$= the productivity of male worker

$\mu 2$= the productivity of female worker

7.1.2 Formulation of Hypotheses in Research:

A. Deductive Method/Approach/Logic: The deductive method is one in which the researcher develops hypothesis from theory and design a research strategy to test them. There, hypothesis formulation is preceded by theory formulation. A clear theoretical portion is developed prior to data collection.

B. Inductive Method/Approach/Logic: The inductive method is in which the researcher develops hypothesis from specific observation. Here, the researcher first collects data and then develops theory as a result of data analysis. It is based on the principle of developing theory after the data have been collected. The two approaches are closely interlinked. Theory and research go side by side. They have never ending interaction. The deductive approach owes more to positivism and the inductive approach to interpretive. However, such labelling is potentially misleading and of no practical value.

7.2 Levels of Measurement in Social Research

The level of measurement refers to the relationship among the values that are assigned to the attributes for a variable. What does that mean? Begin with the idea of the variable, in this example "party affiliation". That variable has a number of attributes. Let's assume that in this particular election context the only relevant attributes are "republican", "democrat", and "independent". For purposes of analyzing the results of this variable, we arbitrarily assign the values 1, 2 and 3 to the three attributes. The level of measurement describes the relationship among these three values. In this case, we simply are using the numbers as shorter placeholders for the lengthier text terms. We don't assume that higher values mean "more" of something and lower numbers signify "less". We don't assume the value of 2 means that democrats are twice something that republicans are. We don't assume that republicans are in first place or have the highest priority just because they have the value of 1. In this case, we only use the values as a shorter name for the attribute. Here, we would describe the level of measurement as "nominal".

7.2.1 Importance of Levels of Measurement: First, knowing the level of measurement helps you decide how to interpret the data from that variable. When you know that a measure is nominal (like the one just described), then you know that the numerical values are just short codes for the longer names. Second, knowing the level of measurement helps you decide what statistical analysis is appropriate on the values that were assigned. If a measure is nominal, then you know that you would never average the data values or do a t-test on the data.

There are typically four levels of measurement that are defined:

1. Nominal.
2. Ordinal.
3. Interval.
4. Ratio.

A. Nominal Scale: In nominal measurement the numerical values just "name" the attribute uniquely. No ordering of the cases is implied. For example, jersey numbers in basketball are measures at the nominal level. A player with number 30 is not more of anything than a player with number 15, and is certainly not twice whatever number 15 is.

B. Ordinal Scale: In ordinal measurement the attributes can be rank-ordered. Here, distances between attributes do not have any meaning. For example, on a survey you might code educational attainment as 0=less than H.S.; 1=some H.S.; 2=H.S. degree; 3=some college; 4=college degree; 5=post college. In this measure, higher numbers mean *more* education. But is distance from 0 to 1 same as 3 to 4? Of course not. The interval between values is not interpretable in an ordinal measure.

C. Interval Scale: In interval measurement the distance between attributes *does* have meaning. For example, when we measure temperature (in Fahrenheit), the distance from 30-40 is same as distance from 70-80. The interval between values is interpretable. Because of this, it makes sense to compute an average of an interval variable, where it doesn't make sense to do so for ordinal scales. But note that in interval measurement ratios don't make any sense—80 degrees is not twice as hot as 40 degrees (although the attribute value is twice as large).

D. Ratio Scale: Finally, in ratio measurement there is always an absolute zero that is meaningful. This means that you can construct a meaningful fraction (or ratio) with a ratio variable. Weight is a ratio variable. In applied social research most "count" variables are ratio, for example, the number of clients in past six months. Why? Because you can have zero clients and because it is meaningful to say that "...we had twice as many clients in the past six months as we did in the previous six months".

It's important to recognize that there is a hierarchy implied in the level of measurement idea. At lower levels of measurement, assumptions tend to be less restrictive and data analyses tend to be less sensitive. At each level up the hierarchy, the current level includes all of the qualities of the one below it and adds something new. In general, it is desirable to have a higher level of measurement (e.g., interval or ratio) rather than a lower one (nominal or ordinal).

8

Review of Literature in Social Research

A literature review surveys scholarly articles, books and other sources relevant to a particular issue, area of research, or theory, and by so doing, providing a description, summary, and critical evaluation of these works. Literature reviews are designed to provide an overview of sources you have explored while researching a particular topic and to demonstrate to your readers how your research fits into the larger field of study.

8.1 Importance of Literature Review

A literature review may consist of simple a summary of key sources, but it usually has an organizational pattern and combines both summary and synthesis, often within specific conceptual categories. A summary is a recap of the important information of the source, but a synthesis is a re-organization, or a reshuffling, of that information in a way that informs how you are planning to investigate a research problem.

The analytical features of a literature review can be as follows:

1. Give a new interpretation of old material or combine new with old interpretations.
2. Trace the intellectual progression of the field, including major debates.
3. Depending on the situation, evaluate the sources and advise the reader on the most pertinent or relevant.
4. Usually in the conclusion of a literature review, identify where gaps exist in how a problem has been researched to date.

8.2 Purposes of Literature Review

1. Place each work in the context of its contribution to the understanding of the research problem being studied.

2. Describe the relationship of each work to the others under consideration.
3. Identify new ways to interpret, and shed light on any gaps in previous research.
4. Resolve conflicts amongst seemingly contradictory previous studies.
5. Identify areas of prior scholarship to prevent duplication of effort.
6. Point the way in fulfilling a need for additional research.
7. Locate your own research within the context of existing literature.

8.3 Types of Literature Review

It is important to think of knowledge in a given field as consisting of three layers. First, there are the primary studies that researchers conduct and publish. Second are the reviews of those studies that summarize and offer new interpretations built from and often extending beyond the original studies. Third, there are the perceptions, conclusions, opinion, and interpretations that are shared informally that become part of the lore of field. In composing a literature review, it is important to note that it is often this third layer of knowledge that is cited as "true" even though it often has only a loose relationship to the primary studies and secondary literature reviews. Given this, while literature reviews are designed to provide an overview and synthesis of pertinent sources you have explored, there are a number of approaches you could adopt depending upon the type of analysis underpinning your study.

8.3.1 Argumentative Review: This form examines literature selectively in order to support or refute an argument, deeply imbedded assumption, or philosophical problem already established in the literature. The purpose is to develop a body of literature that establishes a contrarian viewpoint. Given the value-laden nature of some social science research [e.g., educational reform; immigration control], argumentative approaches to analyzing the literature can be a legitimate and important form of discourse. However, note that they can also introduce problems of bias when they are used to make summary claims of the sort found in systematic reviews.

8.3.2 Integrative Review: Considered a form of research that reviews, critiques, and synthesizes representative literature on a topic in an integrated way such that new frameworks and perspectives on the topic are generated, the body of literature includes all studies that address related or identical hypotheses. A well-done integrative review meets the same standards as primary research in regard to clarity, rigor, and replication.

8.3.3 Historical Review: Few things rest in isolation from historical precedent. Historical reviews are focused on examining research throughout a period of time; often starting with the first time an issue, concept, theory, phenomena emerged in the literature, then tracing its evolution within the scholarship of a discipline. The purpose is to place research in a historical context to show familiarity with state-of-the-art developments and to identify the likely directions for future research.

8.3.4 Methodological Review: A review does not always focus on what someone said [content], but how they said it [method of analysis]. This approach provides a framework of understanding at different levels (i.e. those of theory, substantive fields, research approaches and data collection and analysis techniques), enables researchers to draw on a wide variety of knowledge ranging from the conceptual level to practical documents for use in fieldwork in the areas of ontological and epistemological consideration, quantitative and qualitative integration, sampling, interviewing, data collection and data analysis, and helps highlight many ethical issues which we should be aware of and consider as we go through our study.

8.3.5 Systematic Review: This form consists of an overview of existing evidence pertinent to a clearly formulated research question, which uses pre-specified and standardized methods to identify and critically appraise relevant research, and to collect, report, and analyse data from the studies that are included in the review. Typically it focuses on a very specific empirical question, often posed in a cause-and-effect form, such as "To what extent does A contribute to B"?

8.3.6 Theoretical Review: The purpose of this form is to concretely examine the corpus of theory that has accumulated in regard to an issue, concept, theory, phenomena. The theoretical literature review help establish what theories already exist, the relationships between them, to what degree the existing theories have been investigated, and to develop new hypotheses to be tested. Often this form is used to help establish a lack of appropriate theories or reveal that current theories are inadequate for explaining new or emerging research problems. The unit of analysis can focus on a theoretical concept or a whole theory or framework.

9

Quantitative and Qualitative Research

9.1 Quantitative Research

Different researchers and educators give different definitions to "quantitative research". Here are some of them.

Quantitative research is the numerical representation and manipulation of observations for the purpose of describing and explaining the phenomena that those observations reflect. It is used in a wide variety of natural and social sciences, including physics, biology, psychology, sociology and geology (Wikipedia Encyclopaedia, 2005). In addition, according to Cohen (1980), quantitative research is defined as social research that employs empirical methods and empirical statements. He states that an empirical statement is defined as a descriptive statement about what "is" the case in the "real world" rather than what "ought" to be the case. Typically, empirical statements are expressed in numerical terms. Another factor in quantitative research is that empirical evaluations are applied. Empirical evaluations are defined as a form that seeks to determine the degree to which a specific program or policy empirically fulfils or does not fulfil a particular standard or norm.

Moreover, Creswell (1994) has given a very concise definition of quantitative research as a type of research that is 'explaining phenomena by collecting numerical data that are analyzed using mathematically based methods (in particular statistics)'.

Let's study this definition step by step. The first element is *explaining phenomena.* This is a key element of all research, be it quantitative or qualitative. When we set out to do some research, we are always looking to explain something. In education this could be questions, for example, 'Does constructivism work for teaching English in a Thai context'?, or 'What factors influence student achievement in learning English as a foreign language'?

The specificity of quantitative research lies in the next part of the definition. In quantitative research we collect *numerical data.* This is closely connected to the final part of the definition: analysis *using mathematically-based methods.* In order to be able to use mathematically based methods our data have to be in numerical form. This is not the case for qualitative research. Qualitative data are not necessarily or usually numerical, and therefore cannot be analyzed using statistics.

The last part of the definition refers to the use of *mathematically based methods,* in particular *statistics,* to analyze the data. This is what people usually think about when they think of quantitative research, and is often seen as the most important part of quantitative studies. This is a bit of a misconception. While it is important to use the right data analysis tools, it is even more important to use the right research design and data collection instruments. However, the use of statistics to analyze the data is the element that puts a lot of people off doing quantitative research, because the mathematics underlying the methods seem complicated and frightening.

Therefore, because quantitative research is essentially about collecting numerical data to explain a particular phenomenon, particular questions seem immediately suited to being answered using quantitative methods. For example,

1. How many students learning experiential English I get A's in the first semester?
2. What percentage of the students learning experiential English I has negative attitudes towards the course?
3. On average, is there any significant difference between the general English proficiency of the students learning foundation English and experiential English courses?

These are all questions we can look at quantitatively, as the data we need to collect are already available to us in numerical form. However, there are many phenomena we might want to look at, but which don't seem to produce any quantitative data. In fact, relatively few phenomena in education actually occur in the form of 'naturally' quantitative data.

Luckily, we are far less limited than what might appear above. Many data that do not naturally appear in quantitative form can be collected in a quantitative way. We do this by designing research instruments aimed specifically at converting phenomena that don't naturally exist in quantitative form into quantitative data, which we can analyze statistically. Examples of this are attitudes and beliefs. We might want to collect data on students' attitudes to their school and their teachers. These attitudes obviously do not naturally exist in quantitative form. However, we can develop a questionnaire that asks pupils to rate a number of statements (for example, 'I think school is boring') as either agree strongly, agree, disagree or disagree strongly, and give the answers a number (e.g. 1 for disagree strongly, 4 for agree strongly). Now we have quantitative data on pupil attitudes to school. In the same way, we can collect data on a wide number of phenomena, and make them quantitative through data collection instruments like questionnaires or tests. We will later look at how we can develop instruments for this particular purpose.

The number of phenomena we can study in this way is almost unlimited, making quantitative research quite flexible. However, not all phenomena are best studied using quantitative methods. While quantitative methods have some notable advantages, they also have disadvantages. This means that some phenomena are better studied using qualitative methods.

In short, quantitative research generally focuses on measuring social reality. Quantitative research and/or questions are searching for quantities in something and to establish research numerically. Quantitative researchers view the world as reality that can be objectively determined so rigid guides in the process of data collection and analysis are very important.

9.1.1 Different Types of Quantitative Research: There are several types of quantitative research. For instance, it can be classified as:

1. Survey research.
2. Correlation research.
3. Experimental research.
4. Causal-comparative research.

Each type has its own typical characteristics. Let's take survey research as an example.

Survey research uses scientific sampling and questionnaire design to measure characteristics of the population with statistical precision. It seeks to provide answers to such questions as "How many people feel a certain way"? and "How often do they do a certain behaviour"? Survey research enables management to make comparisons between groups. It provides estimates from a sample that can be related to the entire population with a degree of certainty (e.g., 57 percent of the population +/- 3 percent will answer the question this way 95 percent of the time). Survey research requires that respondents are "randomly" sampled—that means that each person in the population has a known probability of being sampled. There are defined techniques, such as random digit dialling and sampling procedures to ensure a scientific sample. In developing a survey, you would normally work with a statistician to build a statistically valid sampling plan, a researcher to develop a survey instrument and research objectives, and a reputable field service that has the capacity to conduct large scale interview projects. It is important to work with experts because the quality of the survey can be affected by the research instrument.

9.1.2 Common Approaches to Quantitative Research:

1. Surveys.
2. Custom surveys.
3. Mail/e-mail/Internet surveys.
4. Telephone surveys.
5. Self-administered questionnaire surveys.
6. Omnibus surveys.

7. Co-relational research.
8. Trend analysis.
9. Exploratory research.
10. Descriptive research.
11. Experimental research.

9.1.3 Advantages of Quantitative Research: There are many advantages of a quantitative research; these may be outlined as follows:

1. Provides estimates of populations at large.
2. Indicates the extensiveness of attitudes held by people.
3. Provides results which can be condensed to statistics.
4. Allows for statistical comparison between various groups.
5. Has precision, is definitive and standardized.
6. Measures level of occurrence, actions, trends, etc.
7. Can answer such questions as "how many"? and "how often"?

9.1.4 When to Use Quantitative Method? If we take a pragmatic approach to research methods, first of all we need to find out what kinds of questions are best answered using quantitative as opposed to qualitative methods.

There are six main types of research questions that quantitative research is particularly suited to find an answer to:

1. The first is when we want a quantitative answer. For example, 'If the students have their choice, how many of them choose to study experiential English I'? or 'How many English teachers in the language institute would like to teach experiential English courses instead of foundation English courses'? The reason why we need to use quantitative research to answer this kind of question is obvious. Qualitative, non-numerical methods will obviously not provide us with the numerical answer we want.
2. Numerical change can likewise only accurately be studied using quantitative methods. For example, 'Are the numbers of students in our university rising or falling'? or 'Is achievement in English of our students going up or

down'? We would need to do a quantitative study to find out the answer.

3. Quantitative research is useful for conducting audience segmentation. It is done by dividing the population into groups whose members are similar to each other and distinct from other groups. Quantitative research is used to estimate the size of an audience segment as a follow-up step to a qualitative study to quantify results obtained in a qualitative study and to verify data obtained from qualitative study.
4. Quantitative research is also useful to quantify opinions, attitudes and behaviours and find out how the whole population feels about a certain issue. For example, when we want to find out the exact number of people who think a certain way, to set baselines (e.g., to measure consumer attitudes regarding an issue prior to a campaign), and to ensure that the students can share some comments or ideas to a new course.
5. Quantitative research is suitable to explain some phenomena. For instance, 'What factors predict the general English proficiency of the fourth year students?' or 'What factors are related to changes in student English achievement over time'? This kind of question can be studied successfully using quantitative methods, and many statistical techniques have been developed to make us predict scores on one factor or *variable* (e.g. student English proficiency) from scores on one or more other factors or *variables* (e.g. learning habits, motivation, attitude).
6. The final activity for which quantitative research is especially suited is the testing of hypotheses. We might want to explain something, for example whether there is a relationship between students' achievement and their self-esteem and social background.

9.1.5 When Not to Use a Quantitative Method? While quantitative methods are good at answering these four types of questions, there are other types of question that are not well suited to quantitative methods:

1. The first situation where quantitative research will fail is when we want to explore a problem in depth. Quantitative research is good at providing information in breadth from a large number of units. But when we want to explore a problem or concept in depth, quantitative methods are too shallow. To get really under the skin of a phenomenon, we need to go for ethnographic methods, interviews, in-depth case studies and other qualitative techniques.
2. Quantitative research is well-suited for the testing of theories and hypotheses. What quantitative methods cannot do very well is to develop hypotheses and theories. The hypotheses to be tested may come from a review of the literature or theory, but can also be developed using exploratory qualitative research.
3. If issues to be studied are particularly complex, an in-depth qualitative study (a case study, for example) is more likely to pick up on this than a quantitative study. This is partly because there is a limit to how many variables can be looked at in any one quantitative study, and partly because in quantitative research it is the researcher who defines the variables to be studied. In qualitative research unexpected variables may emerge.

Finally, while quantitative methods are better at looking at cause and effect (causality, as it is known), qualitative methods are more suited to looking at the meaning of particular events or circumstances.

9.2 Qualitative Research

Qualitative research is concerned with developing explanations of social phenomena. That is to say, it aims to help us to understand the world in which we live and why things are the way they are. It is concerned with the social aspects of our world and seeks to answer questions about:

1. Why people behave the way they do?
2. How opinions and attitudes are formed?

3. How people are affected by the events that go on around them?
4. How and why cultures have developed in the way they have?

Qualitative research is concerned with finding the answers to questions which begin with: why? how? in what way? Quantitative research, on the other hand, is more concerned with questions about: how much? how many? how often? to what extent? Further features of qualitative research and how it differs from quantitative research are listed below.

Qualitative research is concerned with the opinions, experiences and feelings of individuals producing subjective data. Qualitative research describes social phenomena as they occur naturally. No attempt is made to manipulate the situation under study as is the case with experimental quantitative research.

Understanding of a situation is gained through an holistic perspective. Quantitative research depends on the ability to identify a set of variables.

Data are used to develop concepts and theories that help us to understand the social world. This is an inductive approach to the development of theory. Quantitative research is deductive in that it tests theories which have already been proposed.

Qualitative data are collected through direct encounters with individuals, through one to one interviews or group interviews or by observation. Data collection is time consuming. The intensive and time consuming nature of data collection necessitates the use of small samples.

Different sampling techniques are used. In quantitative research, sampling seeks to demonstrate representativeness of findings through random selection of subjects. Qualitative sampling techniques are concerned with seeking information from specific groups and subgroups in the population.

Criteria used to assess reliability and validity differs from those used in quantitative research.

9.2.1 Features of Qualitative Research: The main features of qualitative research referred to by most writers on the subject (e.g. Grabtree and Miller, 1992; Flick, Kardorff and Steinke, 2000: 24; Lamnek, 1993; Patton, 1990; J.K. Smith, 1990, 1992), can be represented as shown below:

1. **Naturalistic:** It is a research process undertaken in a natural setting (it is field focused).
2. **Dynamic:** It focuses on process and structural characteristics of settings, and trends to capture reality in interaction through intense contact in the field.
3. **Subject-cantered:** It describes life-worlds 'from inside out', from the view of the subjects.
4. **Informative and detailed:** It offers 'thick' descriptions, and allows entry to subjective social construction of people; it presents the information gathered verbally in a detailed and complete form, not in numbers or formulae (no statistical analysis).
5. **Normative:** It employs a value-laden inquiry.
6. **Context-sensitive:** It assumes that the social world is always a human creation, not a discovery.
7. **Reflexive:** It values the reflexivity—the self-awareness—of the researcher.
8. **Open:** It stresses the principle of openness; also, it enters the field with no preconceived ideas or pre-structured models and patterns. There is no strict design; no hypotheses; no limits in its focus, scope or operation.
9. **Flexible:** Design, methods and processes are open to change.
10. **Empathetic:** It aims to understand people, not to measure them.
11. **Communicative:** It focuses on communication which is considered a selective process of meaning production in social contexts. Qualitative research operates within communication, of which it is a part.
12. **Subjective:** It values the subjectivity and the personal commitment of the researcher; it is against objectivity.

13. **Interpretivist:** It values the reflective assessments of the reconstructed impressions of the world.
14. **Holistic:** It focuses on the whole study object in its entirety.
15. **Inductive:** It proceeds from the specific data to general categories and theories.
16. **Small-scale:** It studies a small number of people.

9.2.2 Reasons to Use Qualitative Research

1. To explore a phenomenon that has not been studied before (and that may be subsequently developed quantitatively).
2. To add rich detail and nuance that illustrates or documents existing knowledge of a phenomenon, generated quantitatively.
3. To better understand a topic by studying it simultaneously (triangulation) or concurrently with both methods (mixing quantitative and qualitative methods at the same time or in cycles, depending on the problem).
4. To advance a novel perspective of a phenomenon well studied quantitatively but not well understood because of the narrow perspectives used before.
5. To try to "understand" any social phenomenon from the perspective of the actors involved, rather than explaining it (unsuccessfully) from the outside.
6. To understand complex phenomena that are difficult or impossible to approach or to capture quantitatively.

To understand any phenomenon in its complexity, or one that has been dismissed by mainstream research because of the difficulties to study it, or that has been discarded as irrelevant, or that has been studied as if only one point of view about it was real.

10

Research Design

Research design entails two major stages: one is the stage of planning, and the other is the stage of execution. During the first stage, researchers construct a design, a plan of the research, and during the second they collect and analyze the data. The former is conducted in the researcher's office, the latter in the field. The design explains in some detail how the researcher intends to conduct to conduct the work. This implies that the researcher will go through the research steps, one by one, and describe adequately the activities to be undertaken in each step.

There are many forms of design. Some focus on the process of data collection only (e.g. Diekmann, 1995: 274), while others extend their boundaries to cover data analysis (e.g. Ragin, 1994: 191). Most writers and researchers, however, see the research design in a wider context, covering all aspects of research from collection of data to the publication of the data (e.g. Flick, 2000b).

10.1 Purposes of Research Design

The purpose of research designs varies according to the nature and purpose of the study, the type of population, the structure of the research, the number of researchers ad research assistants, and the ideological affiliation of the researcher, among other factors.

A research design reflects the following list of questions (Berger et al., 1989; Flick, 2000a; Pfeifer, 2000).

1. Offers a guide that directs the research action, and helps to rationalize the use of time and resources, and to reduce costs.
2. Helps to introduce a systematic approach to the research

operation, thereby guaranteeing that all aspects of the study will be addressed and that they will be executed in the right sequence.

3. Entails openness and accountability for research purposes and for the contractors.
4. Helps to control, minimize, or even eliminate eventual influences on data collection and through this on the quality of data.
5. Offers order and clarity on the process of study.
6. Makes the step of the research design clear, enabling the researchers to foresee and prevent eventual errors, bias and distortions.
7. Encourages the effective organization and coordination of the project, particularly when it includes more than one researcher.
8. Makes replication easier and more effective.
9. Enables accurate assessment of the validity and reliability of the study.
10. Enables accurate estimation of the costs of the study and the required personnel.

10.2 Research Design in Quantitative Research

In quantitative research, social inquiry follows a well-constructed design that covers in detail all the steps of the investigation. In this sense, research is perceived as progressing in a sequence of steps that are closely interrelated and develop from the first to the last, and in which the success of each depends on the successful completion of the preceding step.

10.2.1 Features of the Quantitative Research Design:

1. Contains six major steps:

- Selection of topic and methodology.
- Methodological construction of the topic.
- Sampling procedures.
- Data collection.
- Data analysis and interpretation.
- Reporting.

2. Sees the steps as relatively separate and independent parts of the research.
3. Is constructed before the research commences.
4. Is presented precisely in great detail.
5. Is rigid, leaving no flexibility or choice for change during execution.
6. Is a one-way process, allowing no revisiting of steps that have already been completed.
7. Presumes that successful completion of a step depends on the success of previous steps.
8. Is based on objectivity, requiring that all decisions are made using professional standards and allowing no scope for the personal preferences or decisions of the researcher.

10.2.2 Steps in Quantitative Research Design: The following steps are the six major steps in quantitative research design. Each step will be explained in further details in the following paragraphs:

Step 1: Topic and Methodology

- Selection of the research topic.
- Selection of the research methodology.

Step 2: Methodological Construction of the Topic

- Formal definition of the topic.
- Exploration and operationalisation.
- Formulation of hypotheses.

Step 3: Sampling Procedures

- Choice of sampling method.
- Setting administrative parameters.

Step 4: Data Collection

- Choosing the method of data collection.
- Performing/organizing data collection.
- Supervising/checking data collection.

Step 5: Data Analysis and Interpretation

- Analyzing and processing the data.
- Interpreting the findings.

Step 6: Reporting

- Preparing a report for discussion/publication.

These are the major steps in a quantitative research design. The activities of each process have been explained in the following details.

A. Step 1: Topic and Methodology: The research begins with the selection of the research topic to be studied and the research methodology (qualitative or quantitative). At this stage, the researcher makes explicit what is to be studied, and what methodology will be employed.

- **Selection of Research Topic:** Here the topic of the study is formally stated. Any topic that is amendable to social enquiry can be chosen.
- **Selection of Methodology:** The researcher must decide which methodology will direct the study. The choice is usually between quantitative and qualitative research.

For instance, the researcher decides to use a quantitative study, either because this methodology is more suitable for the intended study or because the researcher has already established a methodological affiliation and predisposition to carry out predominantly, or even exclusively, quantitative research.

B. Step 2: Methodological Construct of the Topic: This step aims to make the research topic clear and specific and eventually to reduce it to the actual topic of analysis. In this context the topic will be defined more accurately, explored and operationalized, and hypotheses will be hypotheses will be formulated.

- **Formal Definition of the Topic:** Here, the researcher will explain clearly and accurately the topic as it will be analyzed in the research.
- **Exploration:** This entails a thorough study of existing information on the subject; here the researcher will specify how this will be facilitated.
- **Operationalization:** This entails a process of converting the research topic to a form that can be measured. Operationalization is a process of translating abstract concepts into measurable indicators. Most quantitative

researchers use operational definitions of some kind.

- **Formulation of Hypotheses:** Here the researcher will state whether a hypothesis is required, and if so, which one. (A hypothesis is an assumption about the possible outcome of the study and provides a guideline for the research).

C. Step 3: Sampling: In this part of the design, the researcher will specify where and when the study will be conducted, and who will take part in it, in other words, who will be the subjects.

Sampling is explained in brief in an earlier chapter of this book.

D. Step 4: Data Collection: For this step, the researcher will specify how subjects will be approached, how data collection will be accomplished, and how data will be returned to the researcher. It will also note how research personnel and conditions will be handled so that the data will be gathered without bias and distortion.

E. Step 5: Data Processing: The design will provide how the collected data will be analyzed and processed, including methods of analysis and processing, and the means of accessing the resources required.

For example: Specification of statistical tools to be employed for analyzing the collected data.

F. Step 6: Reporting: In this step, the researcher will specify how the findings will be communicated. This refers not only to the nature of the report but also to the channels of publication.

For example: Who will receive the report, in what form, and in which format it would be written.

10.3 Research Design in Qualitative Research

Qualitative methodology is diverse, pluralistic and in some cases even ridden with internal contradictions (Jacob, 1987; 1988). This is due to the fact that it contains elements from many different schools of thought, which are integrated within this research model. This justifies the belief expressed by some writers that there are not one but many qualitative methodologies and that they cover almost everything in the various qualitative directions in social research (Maindok, 1996: 94). Nevertheless, the central principles of this methodology are taken from a *relativist orientation, a constructive ontology and an interpretivist epistemology.*

Qualitative research employs 'standard' designs and methods as well as projective procedures (Spitznagel, 1991); nevertheless, the methods employed by qualitative researchers are, in most cases at least, those employed by quantitative researchers, adjusted to meet their methodological standards. For example, while both research models employ interviews, quantitative researchers usually employ structured interviews and qualitative researchers', intensive ones. Similarly, while quantitative researchers usually employ structured observation, qualitative researchers employ participant observation.

Qualitative research employ research design as much as quantitative researchers do.. They set the path of their research in some way and form, and are committed to a design, although in their own way (Berg, 1995: 14; Bouma, 2000: 2; Miles and Huberman, 1994:. 16, 17). All know what they intend to study, what settings to investigate how and when, which actors to approach, which processes to consider, what types of events to register and what instruments to employ (Benini, 2000).

The extent to which qualitative designs describe the content of the steps, the degree of rigidity of their instructions and the design of the flow of the research process vary considerably, presenting at least two types of qualitative designs: the *fixed* and the *flexible* designs.

10.3.1 Fixed Qualitative Designs: The fixed model of qualitative design employs a relatively structured approach, resembling the qualitative model. The steps are the same as those of quantitative research, as in the direction of the process, which is a one-way path, from the choice of the topic to the conclusions. Two important points mist be kept in mind when this research model is considered:

First, this model is employed when the researcher has a clear idea about the nature of the research topic and is interested in the way which people respond to it. Hence, methodological parameters can be specified at the outset without knowing the responses of the subjects.

Second, it is employed when data analysis is conducted partly or entirely after data collection. This is, for instance, the case when data are recorded mechanically, and are analysed after collection.

A. Steps in Fixed Qualitative Research Design

Step 1: Topic and Methodology

- Selection of the research topic.
- Selection of the research methodology.

Step 2: Methodological Construction of the Topic

- Framing research questions.
- Literature review; conceptualization.
- Strategy and rationale.

Step 3: Sampling Procedures

- Choice of setting.
- Choice of key informants.
- Choice of study groups and events.

Step 4: Data Collection

- Choice of methods and assistants.
- Entering the setting and conducting research.
- Recording and organizing data.

Step 5: Data Analysis and Interpretation

- Analyzing data.
- Assigning meanings.
- Formulating/testing hypotheses.

Step 6: Reporting

- Preparing a report for discussion/publication.

10.3.2 Flexible Qualitative Research Design: More common is the flexible model of qualitative research design.

The flexible research design:

1. Contains six major steps:
- Selection of topic and methodology.
- Methodological construction of the topic.
- Sampling procedures.
- Data collection.
- Data analysis and interpretation.
- Reporting.
2. Is constructed before the research commences.
3. Is presented in a general and non-specific manner, allowing interpretations, leaving space for further decisions to be considered. Allows freedom of unlimited movement between the steps of data collection and data analysis in both directions, using new information to the fine-tune concepts, sampling and analysis. Qualitative inquiry does not employ a one-way research process.
4. Is not based on objectivity; it follows strictly professional standards; it allows for personal preferences of the researcher.

A. Steps in Flexible Qualitative Research Design

Step 1: Topic and Methodology
- Selection of the research topic.
- Selection of the research methodology.

Step 2: Methodological Construction of the Topic
- Framing research questions.
- Literature review; conceptualization.
- Strategy and rationale.

Step 3: Sampling Procedures
- Choice of setting.
- Choice of key informants.
- Choice of study groups and events.
- Choice of methods and assistants.

Step 4: Data Collection
- Entering field; collecting data; re-defining, aligning methods/sampling; checking for soundness of data.

Step 5: Data Analysis and Interpretation

- Analyzing data.
- Formulating/testing hypotheses.
- Aligning research process.

Step 6: Reporting

- Preparing a report for discussion, submission and publication.

10.4 Four Major Types of Qualitative Research Design

In this section, four major types of qualitative research design are outlined. They are:

1. Phenomenology.
2. Ethnography.
3. Grounded theory.
4. Case study.

Another common research design is the survey. Surveys can be either qualitative or quantitative in their approach to data collection. A description of qualitative surveys can be found in another Trent Focus resource pack.

10.4.1 Phenomenology: The terminology used by different authors can be very confusing and the use of the term *phenomenology* is one example. Phenomenology is listed as one of the terms used to describe qualitative research generally. However, it is also used to describe a particular type of qualitative research.

Phenomenology literally means the study of phenomena. It is a way of describing something that exists as part of the world in which we live. Phenomena may be events, situations, experiences or concepts. We are surrounded by many phenomena, which we are aware of but not fully understand. Our lack of understanding of these phenomena may exist because the phenomenon has not been overtly described and explained or our understanding of the impact it makes may be unclear. For example, we know that lots of people are carers. But what does "caring" actually mean and what is it like to be a carer?

Back pain is another example. Correlation studies may tell

us about the types of people who experience back pain and the apparent causes. Randomised controlled trial of drugs compares the effectiveness of one analgesia against the other. But what is it actually like to live with back pain? What are the effects on peoples' lives? What problems does it cause? A phenomenological study might explore, for example, the effect that back pain has on sufferers' relationships with other people by describing the strain it can cause in marriages or the effect on children of having a disabled parent.

Phenomenological research begins with the acknowledgement that there is a gap in our understanding and that clarification or illumination will be of benefit. Phenomenological research will not necessarily provide definitive explanations but it does raise awareness and increases insight.

10.4.2 Ethnography: Ethnography has a background in anthropology. The term means "portrait of a people" and it is a methodology for descriptive studies of cultures and peoples. The cultural parameter is that the people under investigation have something in common. Examples of parameters include:

- Geographical—a particular region or country.
- Religious.
- Tribal.
- Shared experience.

In health care settings, researchers may choose an ethnographic approach because the cultural parameter is suspected of affecting the population's response to care or treatment. For example, cultural rules about contact between males and females may contribute to reluctance of women from an Asian subgroup to take up cervical screening. Ethnography helps health care professionals to develop cultural awareness and sensitivity and enhances the provision and quality of care for people from all cultures.

Ethnographic studies entail extensive fieldwork by the researcher. Data collection techniques include both formal and informal interviewing, often interviewing individuals on several occasions, and participant observation. Because of this, ethnography is extremely time-consuming as it involves the researcher spending long periods of time in the field.

Analysis of data adopts an "emic" approach. This means that the researcher attempts to interpret data from the perspective of the population under study. The results are expressed as though they were being expressed by the subjects themselves, often using local language and terminology to describe phenomena. For example, a researcher may explore behaviour which we traditionally in the westernized medical world would describe as mental illness. However, within the population under study, the behaviour may not be characterized as illness but as something else—as evidence that the individual is "blessed" or "gifted" in some way.

Ethnographic research can be problematic when researchers are not sufficiently familiar with the social mores of the people being studied or with their language. Interpretation from an "etic" perspective— an outsider perspective—may be a misinterpretation causing confusion. For this reason, the ethnographic researcher usually returns to the field to check his interpretations with informants thereby validating the data before presenting the findings.

10.4.3 Grounded Theory: This methodology originated with Glaser and Strauss and their work on the interactions between health care professionals and dying patients. The main feature is the development of new theory through the collection and analysis of data about a phenomenon. It goes beyond phenomenology because the explanations that emerge are genuinely *new* knowledge and are used to develop new theories about a phenomenon. In health care settings, the new theories can be applied enabling us to approach existing problems in a new way. For example, our approaches to health promotion or the provision of care.

One example of grounded theory with which many of us are familiar is theory about the grief process. Researchers observed that people who were bereaved progressed through a series of stages and that each stage was characterized by certain responses: denial, anger, acceptance and resolution. This is not a new phenomenon, people have going through these stages for as long as society has existed, but the research formally acknowledged and described the experience. Now we use our knowledge of *the grief process*, new knowledge derived from grounded theory, to understand the experience of bereavement and to help the bereaved to come to terms with their loss. We recognize when a person is having difficulty coming to terms with loss because we use the knowledge to recognize signs of "abnormal" grief and can offer help.

Various data collection techniques are used to develop grounded theory, particularly interviews and observation although literature review and relevant documentary analysis make important contributions. A key feature of grounded theory is the simultaneous collection and analysis of data using a process known as constant comparative analysis. In this process, data are transcribed and examined for content immediately following data collection. Ideas which emerge from the analysis are included in data collection when the researcher next enters the field. For this reason, a researcher collecting data through semi structured interviews may gradually develop an interview schedule in the latter stages of a research project which looks very different to the original schedule used in the first interview.

New theory begins its conception as the researcher recognizes new ideas and themes emerging from what people have said or from events which have been observed. Memos form in the researcher's consciousness as raw data is reviewed. Hypotheses about the relationship between various ideas or categories are tested out and construct formed leading to new concepts or understandings. In this sense the theory is "grounded" in the data.

As in phenomenology where there are concepts of which we are aware but do not fully understand, there are aspects of health care which might be informed by the development of new theory. One example is spirituality. In any holistic programme of care health care professionals may talk about the need to meet the "spiritual needs" of patients. However, we understand very little of what this means. At first sight, spiritual needs might be interpreted as referring to religious beliefs but many people would say that spiritual needs are more than this. It may be an individual's sense of well being, happiness or peace of mind. Grounded theory research could provide health care professionals with a better framework for providing truly holistic care.

10.4.4 Case Study: Like surveys, case study research is one of those research approaches which can take a qualitative or quantitative stance. In this resource pack, the qualitative approach to case study is described wherein the value of case study relates to the in depth analysis of a single or small number of units. Case study research is used to describe an entity that forms a single unit such as a person, an organisation or an institution. Some research studies describe a series of cases.

Case study research ranges in complexity. The most simple is an illustrative description of a single event or occurrence. More complex is the analysis of a social situation over a period of time. The most complex is the extended case study which traces events involving the same actors over a period of time enabling the analysis to reflect changes and adjustments.

11

Research Techniques

Research methodology is a way to systematically solve the research problem. It may be understood as a science of studying how research is done scientifically. In it we study the various steps that are generally adopted by a researcher in studying his research problem along with the logic behind them. It is necessary for the researcher to know not only the research methods/techniques but also the methodology. Researchers not only need to know how to develop certain indices or tests, how to calculate the mean, the mode, the median or the standard deviation or chi-square, how to apply particular research techniques, but they also need to know which of these methods or techniques, are relevant and which are not, and what would they mean and indicate and why. Researchers also need to understand the assumptions underlying various techniques and they need to know the criteria by which they can decide that certain techniques and procedures will be applicable to certain problems and others will not. All this means that it is necessary for the researcher to design his methodology for his problem as the same may differ from problem to problem.

In research, the scientist has to expose the research decisions to evaluation before they are implemented. He has to specify very clearly and precisely what decisions he selects and why he selects them so that they can be evaluated by others also. From what has been stated above, we can say that research methodology has many dimensions and research methods do constitute a part of the research methodology. The scope of research methodology is wider than that of research methods.

Thus, when we talk of research methodology we not only

talk of the research methods but also consider the logic behind the methods we use in the context of our research study and explain why we are using a particular method or technique and why we are not using others so that research results are capable of being evaluated either by the researcher himself or by others. Why a research study has been undertaken, how the research problem has been defined, in what way and why the hypothesis has been formulated, what data have been collected and what particular method has been adopted, why particular technique of analyzing data has been used and a host of similar other questions are usually answered when we talk of research methodology concerning a research problem or study.

11.1 Techniques for Quantitative Research

Quantitative methods are generally geared towards documenting subjects attributes expressed in quantity, extent, or strength, as well as guaranteeing—among other things—objectivity, accuracy, validity and reliability. Their purpose is to measure variables and to produces figures which will allow judgments as to the status of the variables in question, which in turn will allow further processing and comparisons and permit replicability.

The most common methods are surveys, documentary methods, observation and experiments. In many instances, quantitative researchers employ qualitative methods in their studies, adjusted to meet the criteria of quantitative research.

11.1.1 Theoretical Background of Quantitative Research: The theoretical underpinnings of quantitative methodology are those of positivism, as guided by a realist and objectivist ontology and an empiricist epistemology. This results in quantitative methodology being an empiricist methodology, and its methods. Its main research parameters are presented below.

A. Perception of Reality: It is characteristic of quantitative methodology that it perceives reality to be objective, simple and fixed. Reality consists of sense impressions, that is, only of what is perceived through the senses; furthermore, there is one reality in nature and only one truth. Reality is independent of human consciousness and rests on order, which is governed by strict, natural and unchangeable laws; knowledge of these laws can help to predict and control the outcomes of human action. All members of society define realty and name them in the same way.

B. Perception of Human Beings: Human beings are rational individuals who are governed by sexual laws; their behaviour is learned through observation and governed by external causes that produce consistent results. Human beings are shaped by their social world just as their physical world is governed by fixed laws; they are subject to fixed patterns of life that are empirically observable. There is no free will. The world is, however, not deterministic; cause produce effects under certain conditions, and predictions can be controlled by the occurrence of such conditions.

C. Nature of Social Science: Here, science, the tool of knowledge extraction is based on strict rules and procedures, and is fundamentally different from speculations, reasons and common sense. Observation and experience offer the basis of knowledge. The task of the scientist/researcher is to discover the scientific laws that explain human behaviour using quantitative methods, similar to those of natural sciences.

D. Purpose of Social Research: The quantitative researcher perceives social research in an instrumental way; research is a tool for studying social events and learning about them and their interconnections so that general causal laws can be discovered, explained and documented. Knowledge of events and social laws allow society to control events and to predict their occurrence and outcomes.

11.1.2 Positivism: Positivism is often taken to be identical to quantitative methodology because it contains the ontological and epistemological prescriptions tat show how this methodology should conduct research. Quantitative research is equally often taken to be identical to positivist research for the same reasons. The nature of this paradigm has already been explained in detail and requires no further discussion. Its elements are reflected in the ontological and epistemological descriptions, as well as in the presentation of the theoretical background of quantitative methodology.

The ten central principles of positivism are:

1. **Objectivism:** Adheres to the notion of objective reality and absolute truths.
2. **Empiricism:** Claims that knowledge comes through sense experience.
3. **Quantitativism:** Stresses the value of accuracy, precision and measurement.
4. **Objectivity:** Discourages subjectivity in the process of social research.
5. **Value-neutrality:** Maintains that facts should be kept apart from values.
6. **Anti-rationalism:** Rejects the notion that knowledge comes from reasons.
7. **Universality of Science:** Asserts that the methods of the physical sciences are applicable also in the social sciences.
8. **Deduction/Induction:** Employs a design based on deduction and produces inductive generalizations.
9. **Determinism:** The world is deterministic, following strict causal laws, and if these laws are discovered social life can be predicted and controlled.
10. **Design:** Employs a strict planned and constructed prior to the commencement of the research.

11.1.3 Central Criteria of Quantitative Research

1. Use of empirical methods.
2. Objectivity.
3. Value neutrality.
4. Clarity in design and procedure.
5. Distance between researcher and subjects of research.
6. Measurement and quantification.
7. Accuracy and precision.
8. Validity and reliability.

9. Reliability.
10. Representativeness and generalization.
11. Strict reliance on methods and their results.
12. Rigorous, disciplined, systematic and reality-bound procedure.
13. Strict research design constructed before research begins.
14. Ethical considerations.

11.2 Techniques for Qualitative Research

Unlike quantitative methodology, qualitative methodology is diverse, pluralistic and in some cases even ridden with internal contradictions (Jacob, 1987; 1988). This is due to the fact that it contains elements from many different schools of thought, which are integrated within this research model. This justifies the belief expressed by some writers that there are not one but many qualitative methodologies and that they cover almost everything in the various qualitative directions in social research (Maindok, 1996: 94). Nevertheless, the central principles of this methodology are taken from a *relativist orientation, a constructive ontology and an interpretivist epistemology.*

Qualitative research employs 'standard' designs and methods as well as projective procedures (Spitznagel, 1991); nevertheless, the methods employed by qualitative researchers are, in most cases at least, those employed by quantitative researchers, adjusted to meet their methodological standards. For example, while both research models employ interviews, quantitative researchers usually employ structured interviews and qualitative researchers', intensive ones. Similarly, while quantitative researchers usually employ structured observation, qualitative researchers employ participant observation.

In the following, the most common and important aspects of qualitative methodology will be introduced.

11.2.1 Theoretical Foundations of Qualitative Methodology

A. Constructionism: Constructionism focuses on the firm belief that there is in practice neither objective reality nor objective truth. On the contrary, reality is constructed. Although physical reality exists, it is not accessible to human endeavour. Constructionism is about realities and relationships (Gergen, 1994; 1999). Trees, rivers, forests and mountains may exist outside people's consciousness but have no meaning before they are addressed by people. Their meaning is not fixed, ready to be discovered—as objectivists propose—but emerges out of people's interaction with the world. Meanings do not exist before a mind engages them. There is no meaning without mind (Cooper, 1998: 8-9).

Constructing reality means making accounts of the world around us and gaining impressions based on culturally defined and historically situated interpretations and personal experiences. This means that what people perceive as reality is not 'the reality', but what they constructed through experiences and interpretations (Lamnek, 1995; Lueger, 2000: 21-38; Luhman, 1997). In this sense, new structures are virtual structures because they do not realize real social phenomena but represent options of expressions of phenomena (Lueger, 2000: 24). They are latent and symbolic. Finally, in the social world there is no single structure but multiple structures interwoven with each other.

It follows that the construction of reality is an active process of creating a world. The reality people experience in everyday life is a *constructed* reality—their reality—based on interpretation. The presence of an objective reality is not disputed here; objective reality exists but it is not accessible. Hence, impressions of reality gained by researchers who listen to respondents talking about their lives are constructions of the constructed reality of the respondents; they are impressions of a reconstructed reality.

For instance, an accident at the street corner is an objective reality, but it is not accessible to researchers. The impressions of witnesses are constructions of what they thought happened. The information gathered by reporters who interviewed these witnesses is a reconstruction of reality, and certainly not 'objective' reality. This allows two major observations. Firstly, there is no single reality but three level of reality; and secondly, reality does not exist in a frozen state; it is marked by a process-nature, recursive and reflexivity. Given also that interpretations vary from one person to another, constructed realities are not uniform. Hence, there are many forms of constructed realities and they therefore cannot be thought of as the only source of knowledge about reality. They are only variants of reality.

Going a step deeper into this process we can say that interpretation and (re)construction allow the identification of meanings assigned to objects, and this leads to a structure of the field. Meanings are employed in the various contexts following cultural instructions than through the labels which, according to objectivists, are attached to objects. Identification of meanings reduces the degree of complexity by replacing this complexity with a new complexity that is easier to explore and understand.

Central to reality construction is 'communication', which is more than a means of exchanging information. Communication is a selective process of producing meaning in social contexts. This process entails three components:

1. Choice of a piece of information.
2. Choice of the form of information that will be shared.
3. Choice of understanding of this information.

Messages are expected to make the content clearly understandable, and to address the point fully. Important in this process of enabling the production of meanings, and of facilitating structuration and communication is, finally, the contextual embedding of objects: objects are meaningful and can be understood only within their context (Lueger, 2000).

B. Interpretivism: The process of construction and reconstruction are laden with personal inputs. Life in a social world makes it necessary for objectivity and rationality to become rather relative concepts. The key process that facilitates construction and reconstruction is *interpretation*. This involves reflective assessment of the reconstructed impressions of the world, and integration of action processes in a general context, which will constitute a new unit.

Interpretivism, as the framework within qualitative research is conducted, 'looks for culturally derived and historically situated interpretations of the social life-world' (Crotty, 1998: 67). It has its roots in the work of Max Weber (1864-1920), which was concerned with *Verstehen* (understanding) of social life, of Wilhelm Dilthey (1833-1911) and of the Neo-Kantian philosophers Wilhelm Windelband (1848-1915) and Heinrich Rickert (1863-1936). *Verstehen* implies an interpretative stance and is contrasted to Erklaren (explaining), which is taken to focus on causality. Within this domain, 'interpretative' means to emphasise the production of meanings and to learn the special views of actors, in other words the local meanings (Pfeifer, 2000).

Verstehen relates to the views, opinions and perceptions of people as they are experienced and expressed in everyday life. Here the qualitative researcher is interested in the subjective meaning, namely the way in which people make sense of their world, and in which they assign meanings to it. The researcher may be interested in what divorce means to children, or in what it means to be a woman working in a job traditionally held by men. Methods commonly used in this context are intensive or narrative interviews and content analysis. An emphasis on the subjective meaning is evident based on symbolic interactionism and phenomenology.

The qualitative researcher often goes beyond identifying the subjective meaning and explores the process of constructing social situation and everyday structures that guide and explain personal views and opinions, and focuses on *the mode of production of social structures.* The researcher is interested here in the factors and conditions, cultural prescriptions and the social order in general that generate certain situations and social structures, for instance, the manner in which structures that oppressed women were created, imposed and maintained. An emphasis on this type of research is evident in paradigms such as ethnomethodology and constructionism.

11.2.2 Central Elements of Qualitative Research: In summary, the following points are most relevant features of the theoretical background of qualitative research.

A. Perception of Reality: Qualitative researchers considers reality to be subjective, constructed, multiple, and diverse. Reality is experienced internally (not through the sense), and resides in the minds of the people who construct it; hence each person constructs his/her own reality, which is therefore subjective. Following this, there are as many realities as there are people, and since people perceive the world in different ways, their realities are different.

B. Perception of Human Beings: In qualitative research, human beings occupy a central position; they create the meaning systems of events and with these they construct reality. They are not non-participant observers but active creators of their world. For most writers on the subject, there are no general laws of a restrictive nature. In spite of this, patterns and regularities of behaviour emerge as a result of social conventions, established through interaction. It is the task of the researchers to search for the systems of meanings that actors use to make sense of their world.

C. Nature of Science: In this context, science as a means of extracting knowledge is assigned a secondary role. Qualitative researchers assert that:

- The basis for explaining and understanding people's life is not 'science', as in quantitative research, but common sense; only this way does it become possible to catch the meanings people use to make sense of their lives.
- The approach employed is inductive, proceeding from the specific to the general and from the concrete to the abstract.
- Science is not nomothetic but ideographic; it presents reality symbolically in a descriptive form.
- Knowledge is not derived through sense experiences only; understanding meanings and interpretations is more important.

- Science is not value free; value neutrality as neither necessary nor possible.

D. Purpose of Social Research: In qualitative research, social inquiry has the purpose of helping the investigators to interpret and understand, first the actors reasons for social action, second, the way they construct their lives and the meanings they attach to them, and third, the social context of social action. What is important here is not observable social action but rather the subjective meaning of social actions.

12

Data Collection and Analysis

Collection of data is of utmost importance for a research investigation. If the data is not accurate or adequate, the findings of the study are bound to be misleading, however, scientific a research might have been. The collection of data depends on the field for which the data should be collected and the methods which are to be used for its collection. The investigator has to decide what methods to use in order to study his problem; whether it is questionnaire, an interview schedule, a case study or observation method or a combination of any of these. The person collecting the data is equally important. He must be unbiased, sharp and courteous to respondents so that they can pleasantly part away with the information.

Collection of data is an essential part of a research proposal. Once the purpose of a statistical investigation has been defined, the problem is to collect data which are relevant to that purpose, to analyse these data and to present them in a meaningful manner.

The nature, purpose and scope of a research study greatly affect the choice of a method to be adopted for the collection of research data. Availability of time and finance also affect the choice of method for the collection of primary data. As the sort of data looked for in qualitative and quantitative researches are different, the methods employed for collection of data also differs across these two types of research.

12.1 Data Collection

Methods of data collection in *quantitative research* are:

1. Observation.
2. Questionnaire.

3. Interview schedule,

Methods of data collection in *qualitative research* are:-

1. Participant observation.
2. Case study.
3. Content analysis.
4. Oral history.
5. Life history.

12.1.1 Data Collection in Quantitative Research: Quantitative inquiries use numerical and statistical processes to answer specific questions. Statistics are used in a variety of ways to support inquiry or program assessment/evaluation. Descriptive statistics are numbers used to describe a group of items. Inferential statistics are computed from a sample drawn from a larger population with the intention of making generalizations from the sample about the whole population. The accuracy of inferences drawn from a sample is critically affected by the sampling procedures used.

It is important to start planning the statistical analysis at the same time when planning for an inquiry begins. Decisions about analysis techniques to use and statistics to report are affected by levels of measurement of the variables in the study, the questions being addressed, and the type and level of information that you expect to include in reporting on your discoveries.

A. Observation Method: Many types of data required by the social scientist as evidence in research can be obtained through direct observation. The great asset of observational techniques is that they make it possible to record behaviour as it occurs. In addition to its independence of a subject's ability to report, observation method is also independent of his willingness to report.

Application of this method in the collection of research data necessitated the identification of sources and fields of investigation. The identification is very important to avoid the likelihood of an investigator to go astray and waste time, effort and scarce funds on unwanted data. After the researcher has satisfied himself about the proper identification of the area of operation, he or his appointed agents collect the data personally by meeting the respondents directly. The researcher or investigation should understand fully the characteristics of the area of operation and should identify himself with the respondents for obtaining correct information. He should be a person of keen observation and should possess a number of qualities. He should be witty, polite, extremely courteous and intellectually very sharp to elicit correct information from the respondents.

However, observation has its specific limitations. This method of collecting primary data is very costly and time consuming. The scope of this method remains limited by the availability of time and funds.

B. Questionnaire and Schedules: A questionnaire is a collection or set of questions. Canvassing schedules and questionnaires have been used for the collection of personal preferences, social attitudes, beliefs, opinions, behaviour patterns, group practices and habits and such other data. The increasing use of schedules and questionnaires is probably due to increased emphasis by social scientists on quantitative measurement of uniformly accumulated data.

(a) Questionnaire: The questionnaires are sent to the concerned persons with the request that the information sought be furnished and the questionnaire returned to the concerned office or agency.

While constructing a good questionnaire the following characteristics may be kept in mind.

1. It deals with a significant topic.
2. It seeks only that information which cannot be obtained from other sources.
3. It is as short as possible, only long enough to get the essential data.
4. It is attractive in appearance, neatly arranged, and beautifully printed.
5. The questions are objective, with no leading suggestions as to

the responses desired.

6. Questions are presented in good psychological order, proceeding from general to specific responses.
7. It is easy to tabulate and interpret.

(b) Interview Schedules: Schedule is the name usually applied to a set of questions which are asked and filled in by an interviewer in a face-to-face situation with another person. Since questionnaires are not an appropriate method for large segments of the population, data can be collected by interviewing almost all segments of the population with the help of schedules.

Following are the merits of interviews:

1. Many people are willing and able to co-operate in a study when all they have to do is talk.
2. Another greater advantage of the interview is its greater flexibility. In an interview there is the possibility of repeating or rephrasing questions to make sure that they are understood.
3. Its flexibility makes the interview a far superior technique for the exploration of areas, where there is little basis for knowing either what questions to ask or how to formulate them.
4. The interviewing situation offers opportunity than the questionnaire to apprise the validity of reports.

12.2 Data Analysis

The methods and techniques of analysis employed by quantitative researchers to analyse data collected through content analysis are many and varied. Examples of some common methods of analysis are given below:

- **Descriptive Analysis:** Here, analysis means counting the frequency of appearance of certain elements of the research question and comparing this with other elements.
- **Categorical Analysis:** Here, analysis involves a study of the documents by means of a set of categories, producing nominal as well as ordinal and interval data, which are

then processed statistically.

- **Valence and Intensity Analysis:** In this form of analysis, data are processed by means of multi-step scales based on the theoretical criteria. In valence analysis the scales have no discrete criteria but have polar values, such as 'in favour of' or 'against'. Intensity analysis employs scales with multiple steps (Lamnek, 1993).
- **Contingency Analysis:** This analysis is basically a semantic communication analysis, usually employed to make an inference from the text about the personality of the author (Merten, 1983).
- **Contextual Analysis:** Here, the sequence in which certain concepts appear together in texts is examined. The systematic co-appearance of certain concepts is not considered to be accidental but is taken to express an author's thinking patterns or to correspond with a speaker's communicative intentions. Such occurrences are thought to signify 'cognitive representations of social reality'.

Quantitative analysis is a diverse and complex process. In the first instance, it entails a primary analysis (dealing with raw data freshly produced by a study), a secondary analysis (involving previously analyzed data), or a meta-analysis. Apart from this, it contains statistical techniques of a varying degree. Statistical processing can be conducted manually or electronically (Rassenberger, 1989; Reid, 1987). Easy access to computers and the many advantages of electronic processing have made this a standard procedure of quantitative analysis. Examples of such advantages are as under:

- Fast data processing and analysis of huge amounts of data.
- Relatively inexpensive data processing and analysis.
- High reliability.
- Accuracy of compensations.
- Accessibility of sophisticated statistical tests to non-statisticians.

12.2.1 Tasks of Quantitative Analysis:

- **Data Preparation:** Checking, editing and coding.

- **Data Entry:** Entering the data in the computer.
- **Graphic Presentation:** For example, presenting the data in the form of graphs or tables.
- **Data Processing and Analysis:** Conducting statistical analysis.
- **Interpretation of the Findings:** Explaining the meaning of data individually.
- **Conclusions:** Proposing direct answers to the research question.

12.2.2 Steps in Quantitative Data Analysis: Data analysis begins where data collection ends; and this is when the instruments of data collection that contain the data (e.g. questionnaires) are completed. From this point on, the researcher will follow a systematic process that begins with preparing the data for computer entry, followed by entering the data in the computer and then by data processing and analysis. The researcher may be interested in getting a brief overview of the general trends regarding the research question. There are many ways of doing this; tables, graphs and statistical coefficients are a few examples. What follows from this stage is interpretation and drawing conclusion.

A. Step 1: Data Preparation: Data preparation first involves checking, editing and coding. Hence, information gathered through the study should be checked and edited so that it is clear, legible, relevant and appropriate. Editing is done where necessary. If answers are missing and/or illegible, the researcher will decide whether to accept or reject them.

Coding is the process of converting verbal responses to numerical codes. For example: 'male may be coded as 1, and 'female' may be coded as 2. Coding can be performed before data collection (pre-coding) or after it (post-coding). The number expressing the codes (e.g. 1 and 2) are called *values,* and the concepts they represent (e.g. 'male' and 'female') the *value labels.*

In quantitative analysis, coding can also be employed when open-ended questions are employed. This involves first the development of categories, and second, the assignment of the corresponding values label and the value to each question. For instance, when the open-ended question deals with the question of how power issues are handled in families, the categories may be 'patriarchal', 'democratic' and 'matriarchal' and the values 1, 2, and 3 respectively. This is followed by a careful reading of the answer, identification of the appropriate category, and entering the corresponding number in the designated place next to the answer. Value labels will be used when entering the data in the computer. Usually, category construction is conducted before the commencement of the study, and the relevant codes are presented in the code book, which is generally made available to coders.

Missing answers to questions or inaccurate responses (e.g., when the tick indicating the gender has been placed ambiguously between 'male' and 'female') must also be recorded. They are called missing values and are represented by '9', '99', or '999', depending on whether the expected value has one, two or three figures.

Finally, investigators are expected to monitor coding in order to prevent errors or bias. Coder reliability is significant and is usually checked in two contexts, the reliability of the coder (i.e., that the coder maintains a stable and uniform pattern of coding, and that variability in coding is avoided) and inter-coder reliability (checked by testing how uniform the pattern of coding is when performed by several coders).

B. Step 2: Data Entry in the Computer: The first step of electronic data processing is to enter the checked and coded answers in the computer. As noted above, for this a computer equipped with the statistical package SPSS Version 10, 11 or 12 (Miller et al., 2002) is required. This program is powerful, student-friendly and relatively inexpensive. The process of entering data in the computer includes two basic steps. These are defining the variables, and entering the data.

12.2.3 Data Analysis in Qualitative Research: The characteristics of qualitative analysis is the it deals with data presented in words; that it contains a minimum of quantitative measurements, standardization and statistical techniques (Engel and Wegging, 1991), and that it aims to transform and interpret qualitative data in a rigorous manner (Coffey and Atkinson, 1996:3). Beyond this, there is simply no consensus as to how qualitative analysis should proceed, or what makes an acceptable analysis. Writer on the subject (e.g. Farber, 2001; Jankowski and Wester, 1991) note that the process of analysis is deeper, more focused and more detailed than in quantitative research, and takes one of two options. These are analytic induction and grounded theory.

Other writers describe further discursive approaches, based on discourse analysis, deconstruction, conversation analysis, dramaturgical analysis, hermeneutic analysis, postmodernist analysis, narrative analysis, semiotics, structuralism and post-structuralism; in brief, qualitative analysis embraces many methods, has many uses, many audiences and many sponsors (Fielding and Lee, 1998). Wolcott, (1992-1994) listed more than 20 research strategies or methods, while Tesch (1990) raises that number to 27. The common elements of those analytic methods are their affiliation with interpretive or hermeneutic paradigms, their understanding of the world as being socially constructed through language, and the notion that analysis deals with the presentation of cultural representations treated as texts (Bennini, 2000; Farber, 2001).

A. Process of Analysis:

In qualitative research analysis researchers:

1. Focus on the gathered data, reading them within the context of the setting and the research purpose, and usually a basic, descriptive content analysis.
2. Identify chunks of data that demonstrates some commonalities and assign them relevant codes.
3. Note thoughts and reflections on parts of data in memos.
4. Work through the materials, to identify patterns, themes, sequences, differences and so on.
5. Construct matrices, network maps, flow charts, diagrams

and other relevant presentation material.

6. Gather new data, and work through it as in previous steps.
7. Establish commonalities and eliminate negative cases, leading to some degree of consistency and to small-scale generalizations.
8. Link generalizations together, testing and re-testing, contrasting, and comparing constantly, leading to typologies and eventually to theories.

B. Varieties of Qualitative Analysis: More specifically, the process of analysis can be categorized in three distinct groups. These are the fixed, the iterative and the subject models of analysis. Briefly, the fixed model is employed when data analysis occurs, after collection, and the iterative model is employed analysis is conducted while collecting data.

The *fixed model* of qualitative analysis deals primarily with written records, that is, with documents. It deals with transcripts which the researcher must read and analyse. In this sense, methods of analysis are those employed when studying documents: document study, content analysis or text analysis.

The *subjective model of qualitative analysis* is diverse and in practice covers whatever does not fit into the other two types of analysis. All these types, however, share a rejection of structured and disciplined models of inquiry, of belief in an ordered world, objective truth or knowledge that can be shared by all academics. Personal choice, decisions and preferences as well as subjective views about truths and knowledge are the basis of this school of thought. Radical postmodernism is an example.

The type of content analysis employed in qualitative research is fundamentally different from that of quantitative studies. The differences relate to theoretical and methodological standards and principles of qualitative analysis, such as openness, communicativity, naturalism and interpretation. Briefly, qualitative data will be analysed as follows: after the units of analysis have been ascertained (e.g. texts or books, transcripts of interviews, or other forms of verbal or visual communication), the researcher will identify and evaluate the items that appear to be theoretically important and meaningful and relate them to the central question of the study. The core of qualitative analysis is in the reconstruction of single cases and the identification of typical structures.

In some cases, the researcher will study the text semantically and systematically, employ the rules of logic, relate the meaning of parts of the texts to the whole document and the general thinking of the author, and develop relevant hypotheses (Danner, 1979; Sofos, 1990). In other cases, the process of collection and analysis of data are seen as an attempt to identify criteria in the text that may refer to actions, effects of expressions and principles that will allow statements about the emotional and cognitive background, as well as about the behaviour of the communicators. Most particularly, Mayring (1983, 1985, 1988, 1991, 2000) proposes that the analysis here will proceed in one of the following ways.

- **Summative Content Analysis:** In this approach data are reduced, so that the text is integrated, important elements are retained and text becomes clear and transparent.
- **Inductive Category Construction:** Here, summarising is taken further, to gradually develop categories from the data. Further analysis of and work with categories allow the construction of overarching categories, and further and research produce the desired answers.
- **Explicating Content Analysis:** This aims at explaining unclear parts of the text (e.g. concepts or sentences). It entails systematic and controlled gathering of extra information. This can be done in two ways, using either information from the same protocol (narrow content analysis), or source outside the protocol (wide content analysis). The important characteristics of explication are its reference to the context; analysis here is explained through the context (in other words, a context analysis).
- **Structuring Context Analysis:** This involves developing structures by putting the material in some kind of order,

for example by means of previously defined criteria (Mayring, 1988: 75). Such structuration may be related to formal criteria (formal structuration), content criteria (content structuration), type of dimensions of criteria (type structuration), or criteria related to0 dimensions of scales (scaling structuration). This eventually leads to the development of dimensions of structuration that can be divided in single categories. This assists with the development of definitions, identification of typical examples and a coding guide, which make the process of structuration more precise.

- **Objective Hermeneutics:** This is a method of content analysis as well as a complete research method. It aims to uncover latent structures of meaning, which lie behind single forms of action and which guide individual action. It is interested in objective and subjective interpretations of social situations, and in the way subjective meanings contrast with the latent structures of meaning (objective interpretations).

C. Main Types of Qualitative Analysis

- **Iterative Qualitative Analysis:** This analytical method employs two major strategies. These are grounded theory and analytic induction. They are characterized by the fact that their analytic process involves repeated use of data collection and analysis.
- **Fixed Qualitative Analysis:** This method of analysis is employed mainly when research followed a fixed research design. In this case, data analysis is conducted after data collection, and the nature of the underlying paradigm.
- **Subjective Qualitative Analysis:** This type of qualitative analysis in effect covers whatever cannot fit into the other two types of analysis. All these types share their relative aversion to structured research and analysis, and a mistrust of strict techniques and methods. In a number of cases, the disbelief on objective truth, as well as in the ability of standard methods to extract knowledge, leads to a

subjective choice of methods that do not rely only on general rules and principles.

13

Experimental Research and Survey

13.1 Experimental Research

It is a collection of research designs which use manipulation and controlled testing to understand causal processes. Generally, one or more variables are manipulated to determine their effect on a dependent variable.

The experimental method is a systematic and scientific approach to research in which the researcher manipulates one or more variables, and controls and measures any change in other variables.

Experimental research is often used where:

1. There is time priority in a causal relationship (cause precedes effect).
2. There is consistency in a causal relationship (a cause will always lead to the same effect).
3. The magnitude of the correlation is great.

The word 'experimental research' has a range of definitions. In the strict sense, experimental research is what we call a true experiment. This is an experiment where the researcher manipulates one variable, and control/randomizes the rest of the variables. It has a control group, the subjects have been randomly assigned between the groups, and the researcher only tests one effect at a time. It is also important to know what variable(s) you want to test and measure.

A very wide definition of experimental research, or a quasi experiment, is research where the scientist actively influences something to observe the consequences. Most experiments tend to fall in between the strict and the wide definition.

A rule of thumb is that physical sciences, such as physics, chemistry and geology tend to define experiments more narrowly than social sciences, such as sociology and psychology, which conduct experiments closer to the wider definition.

13.1.1 Aims of Experimental Research: Experiments are conducted to be able to predict phenomenon. Typically, an experiment is constructed to be able to explain some kind of causation. Experimental research is important to society—it helps us to improve our everyday lives.

After deciding the topic of interest, the researcher tries to define the research problem. This helps the researcher to focus on a more narrow research area to be able to study it appropriately.

The research problem is often operationalized to define how to measure the research problem. The results will depend on the exact measurements that the researcher chooses and may be operationalized differently in another study to test the main conclusions of the study.

Defining the research problem helps you to formulate a research hypothesis, which is tested against the null hypothesis. Conceptual variables are often expressed in general, theoretical, qualitative, or subjective terms and important in hypothesis building process.

An ad hoc analysis is a hypothesis invented after testing is done, to try to explain why the contrary evidence. A poor ad hoc analysis may be seen as the researcher's inability to accept that his/her hypothesis is wrong, while a great ad hoc analysis may lead to more testing and possibly a significant discovery.

There are various aspects to remember when constructing an experiment. Planning ahead ensures that the experiment is carried out properly and that the results reflect the real world, in the best possible way.

13.1.2 Sampling Groups to Study: Sampling groups correctly is especially important when we have more than one condition in the experiment. One sample group often serves as a control group, whilst others are tested under the experimental conditions.

Deciding the sample groups can be done in using many

different sampling techniques. Population sampling may be chosen by a number of methods, such as randomization, "quasi-randomization" and pairing.

Reducing sampling errors is vital for getting valid results from experiments. Researchers often adjust the sample size to minimize chances of random errors.

Here are some common sampling techniques:

1. Probability sampling.
2. Non-probability sampling.
3. Simple random sampling.
4. Convenience sampling.
5. Stratified sampling.
6. Systematic sampling.
7. Cluster sampling.
8. Sequential sampling.
9. Disproportional sampling.
10. Judgement sampling.
11. Snowball sampling.
12. Quota sampling.

The research design is chosen based on a range of factors. Important factors when choosing the design are feasibility, time, cost, ethics, measurement problems and what you would like to test. The design of the experiment is critical for the validity of the results.

Typical designs and features in experimental design are as under:

- **Pre-test-Post-test Design**: Check whether the groups are different before the manipulation starts and the effect of the manipulation. Pre-tests sometimes influence the effect.
- **Control Group**: Control groups are designed to measure research bias and measurement effects, such as the Hawthorne Effect or the Placebo Effect. A control group is a group not receiving the same manipulation as the experimental group. Experiments frequently have 2 conditions, but rarely more than 3 conditions at the same time.

- **Randomized Controlled Trials**: Randomized sampling, comparison between an experimental group and a control group and strict control/randomization of all other variables.
- **Solomon Four-Group Design**: With two control groups and two experimental groups, half the groups have a pre-test and half do not have a pre-test. This is to test both the effect itself and the effect of the pre-test.
- **Between Subjects Design**: Grouping participants to different conditions.
- **Within Subject Design**: Participants take part in the different conditions.
- **Counter-balanced Measures Design**: Testing the effect of the order of treatments when no control group is available/ethical.
- **Matched Subjects Design**: Matching participants to create similar experimental and control groups.
- **Double-Blind Experiment**: Neither the researcher nor the participants know which the control group is. The results can be affected if the researcher or participants know this.
- **Bayesian Probability**: Using Bayesian probability to "interact" with participants is a more "advanced" experimental design. It can be used for settings where there are many variables which are hard to isolate. The researcher starts with a set of initial beliefs, and tries to adjust them to how participants have responded

13.1.3 Pilot Study in Experimental Research: It may be wise to first conduct a pilot-study or two before you do the real experiment. This ensures that the experiment measures what it should, and that everything is set up right.

Minor errors, which could potentially destroy the experiment, are often found during this process. With a pilot study, you can get information about errors and problems, and improve the design, before putting a lot of effort into the real experiment.

If the experiments involve humans, a common strategy is to first have a pilot study with someone involved in the research, but not too closely, and then arrange a pilot with a person who resembles the subject(s). Those two different pilots are likely to give the researcher good information about any problems in the experiment.

A. Conducting the Experiment: An experiment is typically carried out by manipulating a variable, called the independent variable, affecting the experimental group. The effect that the researcher is interested in, the dependent variable(s), is measured.

Identifying and controlling non-experimental factors which the researcher does not want to influence the effects, is crucial to drawing a valid conclusion. This is often done by controlling variables, if possible, or randomizing variables to minimize effects that can be traced back to third variables. Researchers only want to measure the effect of the independent variable(s) when conducting an experiment, allowing them to conclude that this was the reason for the effect.

B. Analysis and Conclusions: In quantitative research, the amount of data measured can be enormous. Data not prepared to be analyzed is called "raw data". The raw data is often summarized as something called "output data", which typically consists of one line per subject (or item). A cell of the output data is, for example, an average of an effect in many trials for a subject. The output data is used for statistical analysis, e.g. significance tests, to see if there really is an effect.

The aim of an analysis is to draw a conclusion, together with other observations. The researcher might generalize the results to a wider phenomenon, if there is no indication of confounding variables "polluting" the results.

If the researcher suspects that the effect stems from a different variable than the independent variable, further investigation is needed to gauge the validity of the results. An experiment is often conducted because the scientist wants to know if the independent variable is having any effect upon the dependent variable. Variables correlating are not proof that there is causation.

Experiments are more often of quantitative nature than qualitative nature, although it happens.

13.2 Survey Research

Survey research is one of the most important areas of measurement in applied social research. The broad area of survey research encompasses any measurement procedures that involve asking questions of respondents. A "survey" can be anything form a short paper-and-pencil feedback form to an intensive one-on-one in depth interview.

We'll begin by looking at the different surveys that are possible. These are roughly divided into two broad areas: Questionnaires and Interviews. Next, we'll look at how you method that is best for your situation. Once you've selected the survey method, you have to construct the survey itself. Here, we will be address a number of issues including: the different types of questions; decisions about question content; decisions about question wording; decisions about response format; and, question placement and sequence in your instrument. We turn next to some of the special issues involved in administering a personal interview. Finally, we'll consider some of the advantages and disadvantages of survey methods.

13.2.1 Types of Surveys: Surveys can be divided into two broad categories: the questionnaire and the interview. Questionnaires are usually paper-and-pencil instruments that the respondent completes. Interviews are completed by the interviewer based on the respondent says. Sometimes, it's hard to tell the difference between a questionnaire and an interview. For instance, some people think that questionnaires always ask short closed-ended questions while interviews always ask broad open-ended ones. But you will see questionnaires with open-ended questions (although they do tend to be shorter than in interviews) and there will often be a series of closed-ended questions asked in an interview.

Survey research has changed dramatically in the last ten years. We have automated telephone surveys that use random dialling methods. There are computerized kiosks in public places that allow people to ask for input. A whole new variation of group interview has evolved as focus group methodology. Increasingly, survey research is tightly integrated with the delivery of service. Your hotel room has a survey on the desk. Your waiter presents a short customer satisfaction survey with your check. You get a call for an interview several days after your last call to a computer company for technical assistance. You're asked to complete a short survey when you visit a web site. Here, we will discuss the major types of questionnaires and interviews, keeping in view that technology is leading to rapid evolution of methods. We'll discuss the relative advantages and disadvantages of these different survey types in advantages and disadvantages of survey methods.

A. Questionnaires: When most people think of questionnaires, they think of the mail survey. All of us have, at one time or another received a questionnaire in the mail. There are many advantages to mail surveys. They are relatively inexpensive to administer. You can send the exact same instrument to a wide number of people. They allow the respondent to fill it out at their own convenience. But there are some disadvantages as well. Response rates from mail surveys are often very low. And, mail questionnaires are not the best vehicles for asking for detailed written responses.

A second type is the *group administered questionnaire*. A sample of respondents is brought together and asked to respond to a structured sequence of questions. Traditionally, questionnaires were administered in group settings for convenience. The researcher could give the questionnaire to those who were present and be fairly sure that there would be a high response rate. If the respondents were unclear about the meaning of a question they could ask for clarification. And, there were often organizational settings where it was relatively easy to assemble the group (in a company or business, for instance).

What's the difference between a group administered questionnaire and a group interview or focus group? In the group administered questionnaire, each respondent is *handed an instrument* and asked to complete it while in the room. Each respondent completes an instrument. In the group interview or focus group, the interviewer facilitates the session. People work as a group, listening to each other's comments and answering the questions. Someone takes notes for the entire group—people don't complete an interview individually.

A less familiar type of questionnaire is the household drop-off survey. In this approach, a researcher goes to the respondent's home or business and hands the respondent the instrument. In some cases, the respondent is asked to mail it back or the interview returns to pick it up. This approach attempts to blend the advantages of the mail survey and the group administered questionnaire. Like the mail survey, the respondent can work on the instrument in private, when it's convenient. Like the group administered questionnaire, the interviewer makes personal contact with the respondent—they don't just send an impersonal survey instrument. And, the respondent can ask questions about the study and get clarification on what is to be done. Generally, this would be expected to increase the percent of people who are willing to respond.

B. Interviews: Interviews are a far more personal form of research than questionnaires. In the personal interview, the interviewer works directly with the respondent. Unlike with mail surveys, the interviewer has the opportunity to probe or ask follow-up questions. And, interviews are generally easier for the respondent, especially if what are sought is opinions or impressions. Interviews can be very time consuming and they are resource intensive. The interviewer is considered a part of the measurement instrument and interviewers have to be well trained in how to respond to any contingency.

Almost everyone is familiar with the telephone interview. Telephone interviews enable a researcher to gather information rapidly. Most of the major public opinion polls that are reported were based on telephone interviews. Like personal interviews, they allow for some personal contact between the interviewer and the respondent. And, they allow the interviewer to ask follow-up questions. But they also have some major disadvantages. Many people don't have publicly-listed telephone numbers. Some don't have telephones. People often don't like the intrusion of a call to their homes. And, telephone interviews have to be relatively short or people will feel imposed upon.

14

Writing a Research Report

A thesis is a written record of the work that has been undertaken by a candidate. It constitutes objective evidence of the author's knowledge and capabilities in the field of interest and is therefore a fair means to gauge them. Although thesis writing may be viewed as an unpleasant obligation on the road to a degree, the discipline it induces may have lifelong benefits.

Most of all, a thesis is an attempt to communicate. Science begins with curiosity, follows on with experiment and analysis, and leads to findings which are then shared with the larger community of scientists and perhaps even the public. The thesis is therefore not merely a record of technical work, but is also an attempt to communicate it to a larger audience.

The structure of a thesis is governed by logic and is invariant with respect to subject. The substance varies with subject, and its quality is determined by the technical knowledge and mastery of essentials exhibited by the student. Style has two components: language and layout. The former deals with the usage of English as a medium of sound technical communication, the latter with the physical presentation of the thesis on paper. All three components—structure, substance and style—influence one another. A good thesis will not be found wanting in any of these three.

14.1 Contents of a Research Report

The content of a research report may be further explained as follows:

14.1.1 Title Page: Title (including sub-title), author, institution, department, date of delivery, research mentor(s) and advisor, their institutions and email addresses.

Table 14.1: Structure of a Research Report

Section	Purpose
Title page	Title of report Student name/student number Course/subject Date due
Table of contents	Shows the sections of the report
Executive summary or abstract	Gives a summary of the whole report Outlines purpose, research method, findings, main conclusions and recommendations Mainly past tense Written last
Introduction	Outlines context, background and purpose Defines terms and sets limits of the research The reader/audience can easily identify what, how, why (Mainly uses past tense and can be written later although presented first)
Methodology	Explains how research was done and outlines how the data was collected
Results/findings may be combined	Presents findings of the research Facts only—no interpretation Uses graphic form (eg. tables and graphs)
Discussion	Presents an interpretation and evaluation of the results. Analyses results—draws together different aspects of the findings, findings of other studies and refers to literature
Conclusion	Brief statement of what was found
Recommendations	Suggest suitable changes/solutions
Appendix	Attachments of additional information (e.g. surveys, questionnaires, glossary etc.)
References	All references used

This may vary among institutions, but as an example: Title/Author/A thesis submitted for the degree of Doctor of

Philosophy in the Faculty of Social Science/The University of Madras/date, month and year.

14.1.2 Table of Contents: The introduction starts on page 1, the earlier pages should have roman numerals. It helps to have the subheadings of each chapter, as well as the chapter titles. Remember that the thesis may be used as a reference in the lab, so it helps to be able to find things easily.

Things to remember while making the table of contents:

- List all headings and subheadings with page numbers.
- Indent sub-headings.

14.1.3 Acknowledgments: Most thesis authors put in a page of thanks to those who have helped them in matters scientific, and also indirectly by providing such essentials as food, education, genes, money, help, advice, friendship etc. *If any of your work is collaborative, you should make it quite clear who did which sections.*

An acknowledgment should express gratitude for the advisor(s) and anyone who helped you in the research process:

1. Technically (including materials, supplies).
2. Intellectually (assistance, advice).
3. Financially (for example, departmental support, travel grants).

14.1.4 List of Tables and Figures: List page numbers of all tables. The list should include a short title for each table but not the whole caption.

List page numbers of all figures. The list should include a short title for each figure but not the whole caption.

While giving the list of figures and list of tables, remember the following:

1. The actual figures and tables should be embedded/inserted in the text, generally on the page following the page where the figure/table is first cited in the text.
2. All figures and tables should be numbered and cited consecutively in the text as figure 1, figure 2, table 1, table 2, etc.
3. Include a caption for each figure and table, citing how it was

constructed (reference citations, data sources, etc.) and highlighting the key findings (think skimming). Include an index figure (map) showing and naming all locations discussed in paper.

You are encouraged to make your own figures, including cartoons, schematics or sketches that illustrate the processes that you discuss.

Examine your figures with these questions in mind:

1. Is the figure self-explanatory?
2. Are your axes labelled and are the units indicated?
3. Show the uncertainty in your data with error bars.
4. If the data are fit by a curve, indicate the goodness of fit.
5. Could chart junk be eliminated?
6. Could non-data ink be eliminated?
7. Could redundant data ink be eliminated?
8. Could data density be increased by eliminating non-data bearing space?
9. Is this a sparse data set that could better be expressed as a table?
10. Does the figure distort the data in any way?
11. Are the data presented in context?
12. Does the figure caption guide the reader's eye to the "take-home lesson" of the figure?

Figures should be oriented vertically, in portrait mode, wherever possible. If you must orient them horizontally, in landscape mode, orient them so that you can read them from the right, not from the left, where the binding will be.

14.2 Introduction

You can't write a good introduction until you know what the body of the paper says. Consider writing the introductory section(s) after you have completed the rest of the paper, rather than before.

What is the topic and why is it important? State the problem(s) as simply as you can. Remember that you have been working on this project for a few years, so you will be very close to it. Try to step back mentally and take a broader view of the problem. How does it fit into the broader world of your discipline?

Especially in the introduction, do not overestimate the reader's familiarity with your topic. You are writing for researchers in the general area, but not all of them need be specialists in your particular topic. It may help to imagine such a person—think of some researcher whom you might have met at a conference for your subject, but who was working in a different area. S/he is intelligent, has the same general background, but knows little of the literature or tricks that apply to your particular topic.

The introduction should be interesting. If you bore the reader here, then you are unlikely to revive his/her interest in the materials and methods section. For the first paragraph or two, tradition permits prose that is less dry than the scientific norm. If you want to be lyrical about your topic, here is the place to do it. Try to make the reader want to read the heavy bundle that has arrived uninvited on his/her desk. Go to the library and read several thesis introductions. Did any make you want to read on? Which ones were boring?

This section might go through several drafts to make it read well and logically, while keeping it short. For this section, I think that it is a good idea to ask someone who is not a specialist to read it and to comment. Is it an adequate introduction? Is it easy to follow? There is an argument for writing this section—or least making a major revision of it—towards the end of the thesis writing. Your introduction should tell where the thesis is going, and this may become clearer during the writing.

Be sure to include a hook at the beginning of the introduction. This is a statement of something sufficiently interesting to motivate your reader to read the rest of the paper, it is an important/interesting scientific problem that your paper either solves or addresses. You should draw the reader in and make them want to read the rest of the paper.

The next paragraphs in the introduction should cite previous research in this area. It should cite those who had the idea or ideas first, and should also cite those who have done the most recent and relevant work. You should then go on to explain why more work was necessary (your work, of course.)

What else belongs in the introductory section(s) of your paper?

1. A statement of the goal of the paper: why the study was undertaken, or why the paper was written. Do not repeat the abstract.
2. Sufficient background information to allow the reader to understand the context and significance of the question you are trying to address.
3. Proper acknowledgement of the previous work on which you are building. Sufficient references such that a reader could, by going to the library, achieve a sophisticated understanding of the context and significance of the question.
4. The introduction should be focused on the thesis question(s). All cited work should be directly relevant to the goals of the thesis. This is not a place to summarize everything you have ever read on a subject.
5. Explain the scope of your work, what will and will not be included.
6. A verbal "road map" or verbal "table of contents" guiding the reader to what lies ahead.
7. Is it obvious where introductory material ("old stuff") ends and your contribution ("new stuff") begins?

Remember that this is not a review paper. We are looking for original work and interpretation/analysis by you. Break up the introduction section into logical segments by using sub-heads.

14.3 Literature Review

Where did the problem come from? What is already known about this problem? What other methods have been tried to solve it?

Ideally, you will already have much of the hard work done, if you have been keeping up with the literature as you vowed to do three years ago, and if you have made notes about important papers over the years. If you have summarized those papers, then you have some good starting points for the review.

If you didn't keep your literature notes up to date, you can still do something useful: pass on the following advice to any beginning Ph.D. students in your lab and tell them how useful this would have been to you. When you start reading about a topic, you should open a spread sheet file, or at least a word processor file, for your literature review. Of course you write down the title, authors, year, volume and pages. But you also write a summary (anything from a couple of sentences to a couple of pages, depending on the relevance). In other columns of the spread sheet, you can add key words (your own and theirs) and comments about its importance, relevance to you and its quality.

How many papers? How relevant do they have to be before you include them? Well, that is a matter of judgment. On the order of a hundred is reasonable, but it will depend on the field. You are the world expert on the (narrow) topic of your thesis: you must demonstrate this.

A political point: make sure that you do not omit relevant papers by researchers who are like to be your examiners, or by potential employers to whom you might be sending the thesis in the next year or two.

14.4 Research Methodology

14.4.1 Materials and Methods: This varies enormously from thesis to thesis, and may be absent in theoretical theses. It should be possible for a competent researcher to reproduce exactly what you have done by following your description. There is a good chance that this test will be applied: sometime after you have left, another researcher will want to do a similar experiment either with your gear, or on a new set-up in a foreign country. Please write for the benefit of that researcher.

In some thesis, particularly multi-disciplinary or developmental ones, there may be more than one such chapter. In this case, the different disciplines should be indicated in the chapter titles.

14.4.2 Theory: When you are reporting theoretical work that is not original, you will usually need to include sufficient material to allow the reader to understand the arguments used and their physical bases. Sometimes you will be able to present the theory *ab initio,* but you should not reproduce two pages of algebra that the reader could find in a standard text. Do not include theory that you are not going to relate to the work you have done.

When writing this section, concentrate at least as much on the physical arguments as on the equations. What do the equations mean? What are the important cases?

When you are reporting your own theoretical work, you must include rather more detail, but you should consider moving lengthy derivations to appendices. Think too about the order and style of presentation: the order in which you did the work may not be the clearest presentation.

Suspense is not necessary in reporting science: you should tell the reader where you are going before you start.

Contents of a "methodology" section of a scientific paper should be as under:

1. Information to allow the reader to assess the believability of your results.
2. Information needed by another researcher to replicate your experiment.
3. Description of your materials, procedure, theory.
4. Calculations, technique, procedure, equipment, and calibration plots.
5. Limitations, assumptions, and range of validity.
6. Description of your analytical methods, including reference to any specialized statistical software.

The methods section should answer the following questions and caveats:

1. Could one accurately replicate the study (for example, all of the optional and adjustable parameters on any sensors or instruments that were used to acquire the data)?
2. Could another researcher accurately find and reoccupy the sampling stations or track lines?
3. Is there enough information provided about any instruments used so that a functionally equivalent instrument could be used to repeat the experiment?
4. If the data are in the public domain, could another researcher lay his or her hands on the identical data set?
5. Could one replicate any laboratory analyses that were used?
6. Could one replicate any statistical analysis?
7. Could another researcher approximately replicate the key algorithms of any computer software?
8. Citations in this section should be limited to data sources and references of where to find more complete descriptions of procedures.
9. Do not include descriptions of results.

14.4.3 Results:

1. The results are actual statements of observations, including statistics, tables and graphs.
2. Indicate information on range of variation.
3. Mention negative results as well as positive. Do not interpret results—save that for the discussion.
4. Lay out the case as for a jury. Present sufficient details so that others can draw their own inferences and construct their own explanations.
5. Use S.I. units (m, s, kg, W, etc.) throughout the thesis.
6. Break up your results into logical segments by using subheadings

Key results should be stated in clear sentences at the beginning of paragraphs. It is far better to say "X had significant positive relationship with Y (linear regression p<0.01, r^2=0.79)" then to start with a less informative like "There is a significant relationship between X and Y". Describe the nature of the findings; do not just tell the reader whether or not they are significant.

14.4.4 Results vs. Discussion Sections: Quarantine your observations from your interpretations. The writer must make it crystal clear to the reader which statements are observation and which are interpretation. In most circumstances, this is best accomplished by physically separating statements about new observations from statements about the meaning or significance of those observations. Alternatively, this goal can be accomplished by careful use of phrases such as "I infer..." vast bodies of geological literature became obsolete with the advent of plate tectonics; the papers that survived are those in which observations were presented in stand-alone fashion, unmuddied by whatever ideas the author might have had about the processes that caused the observed phenomena.

This can be done by the following steps:

1. Physical separation into different sections or paragraphs.
2. Don't overlay interpretation on top of data in figures.
3. Careful use of phrases such as "we infer that".
4. Don't worry if "results" seem short.

14.5 Discussion

Start with a few sentences that summarize the most important results. The discussion section should be a brief essay in itself, answering the following questions and caveats:

1. What are the major patterns in the observations? (Refer to spatial and temporal variations.)
2. What are the relationships, trends and generalizations among the results?
3. What are the exceptions to these patterns or generalizations?
4. What are the likely causes (mechanisms) underlying these patterns resulting predictions?
5. Is there agreement or disagreement with previous work?
6. Interpret results in terms of background laid out in the

introduction—what is the relationship of the present results to the original question?

7. What is the implication of the present results for other unanswered questions in earth sciences, ecology, environmental policy etc.?
8. Multiple hypotheses: There are usually several possible explanations for results. Be careful to consider all of these rather than simply pushing your favourite one. If you can eliminate all but one, that is great, but often that is not possible with the data in hand. In that case you should give even treatment to the remaining possibilities, and try to indicate ways in which future work may lead to their discrimination.
9. Avoid bandwagons: A special case of the above. Avoid jumping a currently fashionable point of view unless your results really do strongly support them.
10. What are the things we now know or understand that we didn't know or understand before the present work?
11. Include the evidence or line of reasoning supporting each interpretation.
12. What is the significance of the present results: why should we care?

This section should be rich in references to similar work and background needed to interpret results. However, interpretation/discussion section(s) are often too long and verbose. Is there material that does not contribute to one of the elements listed above? If so, this may be material that you will want to consider deleting or moving. Break up the section into logical segments by using subheads.

14.6 Recommendations

It is often the case with scientific investigations that more questions than answers are produced. Does your work suggest any interesting further avenues? Are there ways in which your work could be improved by future workers? What are the practical implications of your work?

This chapter should usually be reasonably short—a few pages perhaps.

Things to remember while writing this segment of a research report:

1. Include when appropriate (most of the time).
2. Remedial action to solve the problem.
3. Further research to fill in gaps in our understanding.
4. Directions for future investigations on this or related topics.

14.7 References

A reference section highlights all the sources of readily available information, such as books, journals, and newspapers etc., which were used in the research.

It is tempting to omit the titles of the articles cited, and the universities allows this, but think of all the times when you have seen a reference in a paper and gone to look it up only to find that, it was not helpful after all.

Should you reference websites and, if so, how? If you cite a journal article or book, the reader can go to a library and check that the cited document and check whether or not it says what you say it did. A web site may disappear, and it may have been updated or changed completely. So references to the web are usually less satisfactory. Nevertheless, there are some very useful and authoritative sources. So, if the rules of your institution permit it, it may be appropriate to cite web sites. (Be cautious, and don't overuse such citations. In particular, don't use a web citation where you could reasonably use a "hard" citation. Remember that your examiners are likely to be older and more conservative.) You should give the URL and also the date you downloaded it. If there is a date on the site itself (last updated on...) you should include that, too.

The major things to remember while writing a reference section may be explained as follows:

1. Cite all ideas, concepts, text, data that are not your own.

2. If you make a statement, back it up with your own data or a reference.
3. All references cited in the text must be listed.
4. Cite single-author references by the surname of the author (followed by date of the publication in parenthesis).

- ...according to Hays (1994).
- ...population growth is one of the greatest environmental concerns facing future generations (Hays, 1994).

5. Cite double-author references by the surnames of both authors (followed by date of the publication in parenthesis)

- e.g. Simpson and Hays (1994).

6. Cite more than double-author references by the surname of the first author followed by et al. and then the date of the publication.

- e.g. Pfirman, Simpson and Hays would be: Pfirman et al. (1994).

7. Do not use footnotes.
8. List all references cited in the text in alphabetical order using the following format for different types of material:

- Hunt, S. (1966) Carbohydrate and amino acid composition of the egg capsules of the whelk. *Nature*, 210, 436-437.
- National Oceanic and Atmospheric Administration (1997) Commonly asked questions about ozone. http://www.noaa.gov/public-affairs/grounders/ozo1.htnl, 9/27/97.
- Pfirman, S.L., M. Stute, H.J. Simpson, and J. Hays (1996), Undergraduate research at Barnard and Columbia, *Journal of Research*, 11, 213-214.
- Pechenik, J.A. (1987), A Short Guide to Writing About Biology. Harper Collins Publishers, New York, 194 pp.
- Pitelka, D.R., and F.M. Child (1964), Review of Ciliary Structure and Function. In, *Biochemistry and Physiology of Protozoa*, Vol. 3 (S.H. Hutner, editor), Academic Press, New York, 131-198.
- Sambrotto, R. (1997), lecture notes, Environmental Data Analysis, Barnard College, October 2, 1997.

- Stute, M., J.F. Clark, P. Schlosser, W.S. Broecker, and G. Bonani (1995), A high altitude continental paleotemperature record derived from noble gases dissolved in groundwater from the San Juan Basin, New Mexico. *Quat. Res.*, 43, 209-220.
- New York Times (1/15/00) PCBs in the Hudson still an issue, A2.

It is acceptable to put the initials of the individual authors behind their last names, e.g. Pfirman, S.L., Stute, M., Simpson, H.J., and Hays, J. (1996), Undergraduate research at...

14.8 Appendices

If there is material that should be in the thesis but which would break up the flow or bore the reader unbearably, include it as an appendix.

Some things which are typically included in appendices are: important and original computer programs, data files that are too large to be represented simply in the results chapters, pictures or diagrams of results which are not important enough to keep in the main text.

Things to remember while preparing the appendix section:

1. Include all your data in the appendix.
2. Reference data/materials not easily available (theses are used as a resource by the department and other students).
3. Tables (where more than 1-2 pages).
4. Calculations (where more than 1-2 pages).
5. You may include a key article as appendix.
6. If you consulted a large number of references but did not cite all of them, you might want to include a list of additional resource material, etc.
7. List of equipment used for an experiment or details of complicated procedures.

Note: Figures and tables, including captions, should be embedded in the text and not in an appendix, unless they are more than 1-2 pages and are not critical to your argument.

14.9 Editing Your Thesis

Even a rough draft of a thesis should be edited.

14.9.1 Copy Editing:

1. Proof read your thesis a few times.
2. Check your spelling. Spellcheckers are useful for initial checking, but don't catch homonyms (e.g. hear, here), so you need to do the final check by eye.
3. Make sure that you use complete sentences.
4. Check your grammar: punctuation, sentence structure, subject-verb agreement (plural or singular), tense consistency, etc.
5. Give it to others to read and comment.

14.9.2 Content Editing: Following are the kind of things to check in a content editing:

1. Logic.
2. Repetition, relevance.
3. Style.

14.9.3 Avoiding Ambiguity:

1. Do not allow run-on sentences to sneak into your writing; try semicolons.
2. Avoid nested clauses/phrases.
3. Avoid clauses or phrases with more than two ideas in them.
4. Do not use double negatives.
5. Do not use dangling participles (i.e. phrases with an "-ing" verb, in sentences where the agent performing the action of the "-ing" verb is not specified: "After standing in boiling water for two hours, examine the flask").
6. Make sure that the antecedent for every pronoun (it, these, those, that, this, one) is crystal clear. If in doubt, use the noun rather than the pronoun, even if the resulting sentence seems a little bit redundant.
7. Ensure that subject and verb agree in number (singular versus plural).
8. Be especially careful with compound subjects. Be especially careful with subject/verb agreement within clauses.

9. Avoid qualitative adjectives when describing concepts that are quantifiable ("The water is deep". "Plate convergence is fast". "Our algorithm is better"). Instead, quantify. ("Water depths exceed 5 km.").
10. Avoid noun strings ("acoustic noise source location technique").
11. Do not use unexplained acronyms. Spell out all acronyms the first time that you use them.

14.10 Language in Writing a Thesis

Language is one aspect of a thesis writing that attracts little attention but is crucial to excellent thesis writing. Use of nouns, adjectives, clauses, passive and active voices, use of abbreviations, and symbols are some of the aspect of language that needs careful consideration while writing a thesis.

Now, let us see this aspect of language in thesis writing:

14.10.1 Clusters of Nouns: When clustered together, all nouns except the last function as adjectives. Avoid expressions like "chemical healing suppression" and say instead, "suppression of healing by chemicals", or "suppression of chemical healing", or whatever else you intended to mean. Use prepositions to make your meaning clear.

14.10.2 Adjectival Clauses: Instead of "an innovation based return on investment culture", say "a culture of innovation based on return-on-investment" or whatever you actually meant to say. Again, use prepositions to make your meaning clear, even if this construction is longer.

14.10.3 Subordinate Clauses at the Beginning: This style puts the unimportant bits first and the important ones later. It may be good electronics to do so (LSB14 first), but it is bad English. Avoid beginning sentences with constructions like "Despite the fact that...", "Notwithstanding the fact that...", etc. Compare these two versions:

Thus, although there were too few plots15 to show all of the interactions which we sought [subordinate clause, apologetic], under the conditions of the experiment [subordinate phrase, conditional], copper and zinc acted additively. Thus, copper and zinc acted additively under the conditions of our experiment, although there were...The second sentence certainly reads better. It is also a good example of putting the important information in the topic position.

Avoid writing "Recording of pulse rates was made"; instead write, "Pulse rates were recorded". We have improved the original sentence in three ways by doing this. We have:

- Replaced the original dummy verb "made" with the genuine verb "recorded";
- Shortened the sentence; and
- Sharpened the impact.

14.10.4 Use of Filler Verbs: Do not write "We conducted a study of group III-V compounds"; instead say, "We studied group III-V compounds". The second sentence has five words; the first, eight. Again, a dummy verb has been replaced with a genuine verb and the sentence has been shortened and strengthened. Examples of dummy verb constructions to be avoided are "to be present", "to occur", "to perform", "to obtain" etc.

14.10.5 Use of Passive Voice Rather than Active Voice. Passive voice is appropriate when the doer of an action is unknown or is irrelevant. Otherwise, passive voice lengthens and weakens the sentence, whereas active voice is direct, succinct and more forceful. Compare "Patients were observed by two people for signs of abnormal behaviour" [5, p. 49] with "Two people observed the patients..." [5, p. 49].

14.10.6 Use of Imprecise Words: Do not use words like "quite", "some", "considerable", "a great deal", etc. in scientific writing. It is imprecise and unhelpful to the reader.

Be quantitative: you are writing an engineering thesis. Sometimes, you may wish to avoid numerical precision for some compelling reason. If you want to avoid writing "Fifty-two percent of the images were correctly classified", do not say "The majority of the images were correctly classified", but rather "Slightly over half the images were correctly classified".

14.10.7 Use of Compound Prepositions: Debaters and politicians use expressions like "in the case of", "in respect of", etc., usually to gain time to think of a proper answer during a debate or a press conference. Such expressions dilute the force of the simple, direct statement: they have no place in your thesis.

14.10.8 Multiple Negatives: A double negative, when used carefully, has impact or conveys just the right shade of meaning. Multiple negatives do not. They serve only to confuse and should be avoided. What does "not unreasonably inefficient" really mean? Anytime you cause your reader to backtrack or pause for mental breath to take in meaning, you have done yourself and your reader a disservice.

14.10.9 Unfamiliar Abbreviations and Symbols: Stick to SI units and prefixes. If you have to introduce a new unit called a flip make sure that you define it somewhere, introduce an abbreviation consistent with the SI system, use SI prefixes, and stick with your nomenclature all through.

14.10.10 Punctuation: Good punctuation makes reading easy. The simplest way to find out where to punctuate is to read aloud what you have written. Each time you pause, you should add a punctuation symbol. There are four major pause symbols, arranged below in ascending order of "degree of pause":

14.10.11 Comma, Semi-colon, Colon: Use the comma to indicate a short pause or to separate items in a list. A pair of commas may delimit the beginning and end of a subordinate clause or phrase. Sometimes, this is also done with a pair of "em dashes" which are printed like this:

The semi-colon signifies a longer pause than the comma. It separates segments of a sentence that are "further apart" in position, or meaning, but which are nevertheless related. If the ideas were "closer together", a comma would have been used. It is also used to separate two clauses that may stand on their own but which are too closely related for a colon or full stop to intervene between them.

The colon is used before one or more examples of a concept, and whenever items are to be listed in a visually separate fashion. The sentence that introduced the itemized list you are now reading ended in a colon. It may also be used to separate two fairly—but not totally—independent clauses in a sentence.

14.10.12 Full Stop or Period: The full stop ends a sentence. If the sentence embodies a question or an exclamation, then, of course, it is ended with a question mark or exclamation mark, respectively. The full stop is also used to terminate abbreviations like etc., (for• et cetera), e.g., for (exempli gratia), et al., (for et alia) etc., but not with abbreviations for SI units.

14.11 Citing Sources in Scholarly Communication

Introduction: This chapter presents the basic guidelines for citing sources following the University of Chicago Press's *Chicago Manual of Style* and Kate L. Turabian's *A Manual for Writers of Term Papers, Theses, and Dissertations,* commonly referred to as Chicago Style or Turabian Style with examples.

14.11.1 Rules Governing in Chicago and Turabian Style: The rules governing in Chicago and Turabian Style general rules for citing information sources is as follows:

- **General:** List the elements that clearly identify the work's author and title, its publisher, and date of publication. For online publications, add elements stating where you retrieved the document and the date accessed, if required.
- **Punctuation:** Periods are generally used between elements in references in bibliographies and reference lists. A colon separates titles from subtitles, the place of publication from the publisher name, and volume information from page numbers for journal articles. Quotation marks are used around article and chapter titles.
- **Capitalization**: In bibliographies and notes, capitalize the first letter of all significant words in titles and subtitles of works and parts of works such as articles or chapters. In

reference lists, capitalize the first letter of all significant words only in titles of periodicals, and capitalize only the first letter of the first word (and any proper nouns) of titles and subtitles of articles, books, and chapters, and corporate authors.

- **Font:** Italicize titles of periodicals and books.
- **Abbreviations:** Use ed. or trans. for "editor" or "edited by" or "translator" or "translated by". "University" may be abbreviated to Univ. Months may be abbreviated. Be consistent throughout your paper with whatever conventions you adopt.
- **Footnotes and Endnotes:** Number notes consecutively throughout your paper, beginning with one. Format is the same for endnotes and footnotes. Endnotes should follow the body of the paper and precede any appendices and the bibliography. In Turabian style, use superscript [1] for endnote and footnote numbers in the text and at the beginning of each note. In Chicago style, the note number in the text is in parentheses (1) and is followed by a period and space in the note: 1. Note content.
- **Authors' Names:** In bibliographies and reference lists, only the first author's last name is inverted (last name first). First names should usually be provided when available. List all authors' names in a bibliography or reference list. In in-text parenthetical references, list the last names of one to three authors; if more than three, list the first followed by et al. Corporate names as authors are written out.
- **Publication Place:** If more than one place is given, the first is generally sufficient. Do not abbreviate place names. Give the city and state or country if the city is not well known for publishing or is ambiguous.
- **Publisher:** Provide the exact publisher name. Common names may be shortened (e.g., Scribner, Macmillan).
- **Publication Date:** In notes and bibliographies, the date of publication for books and most published works follows

the publisher name. For articles, it is part of the volume and issue number statement (below). In reference lists, the year of publication immediately follows the name(s) of the author(s). For works with no author or editor, put the title first and follow it by the year of publication. If there is no date available, state: n.d.

- **Volume and Issue Numbers:** For periodicals with continuous pagination throughout a volume, provide only the volume number and year. If issue begins with page 1, follow the volume number with the issue number identified by "no." or its name: 38, no. 2 (1993): 12-17.
- **Electronic Resources.** Follow rules that apply to equivalent parts of print resources as much as possible. When in doubt, avoid italics and quotation marks and give as much information as may be useful. Too much is better than too little.

15

Problems in the Study of Social Phenomena

Research in social sciences is the direct outcome of man's urge to understand his society, its nature and working. Social phenomena play a crucial role in the direction and depth of social research. Because of the inherent ambiguities and uniqueness of social phenomena, difficulties often arise as to the precise measure of social investigation. Human beings do not operate under controlled conditions; on the contrary they are always under the diverse influences such as environmental, psychological and social and these influences freely interact with each other and seldom operate in isolation. This interplay of diverse influences makes social phenomena complex. The complexity is further accentuated by the uniqueness of each individual's behaviour. No two persons look alike in thinking, working and attitudes. In a huge societal laboratory it is hard to conduct precise experiments.

The problem of heterogeneity is sought to be solved by proper stratification and classification of social phenomena. Within each situation, greater homogeneity is ensured. Even though research under controlled condition is not possible, greater homogeneity at micro-level has improved the quality of social research significantly. Research in physical sciences is older than that in the social sciences and has, therefore, attained greater maturity. If the current rate of progress in social research continues, things will certainly improve further. Though man can never perform as machine skilfulness will certainly enable him to work with more advanced machinery to the benefit of entire human community.

The problems in the study of social phenomena are broadly described as:

1. Subjectivity

2. Objectivity.

The above terms may be explained further as follows.

15.1 Subjectivity

To make guidelines serve as more than wishful thinking, someone must back them up by sanctions and external reviewers. For example, a postulate of the Nuremberg Code permits a degree of risk to the subject up to the "humanitarian importance of the problem". This guideline, if left to the researcher could lead to the subjective overvaluing of the "importance" of the study and/or undervaluing of the subject's risk.

Two general enforcement approaches to these ethical principles exists. The first tries to discourage violations of ethical guidelines through penalties. The second uses prior review of research proposals to deny resources for unethical research.

15.1.1 Punishing Human Subject Violations: Remedies. All citizens enjoy the protection of their lives and liberty to the extent guaranteed by state and federal laws. Suppose a demented social researcher physically pulls you off the street and forces you to serve as subject. In this case you can look to the criminal justice system for the punishment of this violation of the kidnapping laws.

However, you are much more likely to encounter unethical research that comes under the civil code. As one example, the Tuskegee Study ultimately concluded with an out-of-court financial settlement of a class action civil suit. The federal government agreed to pay the subjects for their physical and mental stress. Similarly, every social researcher stands liable to lawsuit by human subjects who feel mistreated. Although rare, such suits provide one check on researchers.

Both criminal and civil law provide two essential ingredients for punishment. First, a formal and neutral judge or jury decides whether someone has violated a law or caused a personal injury. Second, the law can levy a financial or other penalty. However, before this judicial process can operate, someone must file a complaint. As shown by the Tuskegee Study, making effective use of the legal system will often prove difficult for the least powerful subjects. In that case, civil action derived not from the subjects but rather from civil rights activists outraged by the study. In less extreme cases of abuse, even well-informed and resourceful subjects may decide that the cost of seeking legal redress exceeds the discomfort caused by their research experience.

15.1.2 Professional Associations: To provide protection of human subjects while maximizing the freedom of their members, professional associations and universities offer an alternative outside the legal system. Most social research organizations provide their member with ethical guidelines. Anyone, including research subjects or other professionals, can call attention to violations of these guidelines. Indeed the members of these associations have an obligation not only to adhere to their group's standards but also to see that their fellow members adhere to them as well. These organizations and their members can enforce their principles in various ways. Most of these associations own journals and can deny publication of research reports based in unethical treatment of human subjects. Some associations issue public reprimands to unethical members, which can threaten their continued employment and funding. The ultimate sanction that such voluntary groups can impose is removal from the membership.

The human subject portions of the ethical guidelines illustrate the similarities and differences across different disciplines. Anthropologists' wide use of field observation methods creates special concern for their key informants and the protection of the general population being studied (often minority or Third World cultures). Psychologists' extensive use of experimental design explains their special concern with such matters as deception. Psychologists also sometimes use animals in their research, and these subjects are also protected in the American Psychological Association's ethical guidelines. Sociologists' frequent use of archival records and surveys accounts for their emphasis on matters related to confidentiality.

Ideally, scholars will learn and internalize the guidelines detailed in these tables and in turn identify and eliminate threats to human subjects. Sadly, not all members of a discipline obey these codes. Moreover, some of these principles seem unclear. As a result, professional associations sometimes need procedures to clarify and enforce their rules.

For example, the American Psychological Associations (APA) has an Ethic Committee that reviews complaints about APA members and reports to the membership on trends in these complaints and their adjudication. Such complaints have increased from an average of about 57 in the 3½ years up to 1980 (Sanders and Keith-Spielgel, 1980) to 88 per year in 1986 and 1987 (Ethics Committee of the American Psychological Association, 1988). However, most of these ethical cases involve issues outside the research domain. The Ethics Committee opened only 3 cases regarding improper research techniques in the year 1990 through 1992 out of 264 total cases in those years (Ethics Committee of the American Psychological Association, 1993).

Given the large membership of APA (over 72, 644 in 1992) and the relatively intrusive nature of many psychological experiments, this record suggests little need for concern. However, another report based on a large sample (n = 19, 000) of the membership yielded 5,000 descriptions of ethically troubled human research studies (Ad Hoc Committee on Ethical Standards in Psychological Research, 1973). The number and severity of these descriptions suggests that the Association's Ethics Committee may fail to hear many violations. Some psychologists may refuse to report fellow psychologists for ethics violations. The percentage of complaints to the APA filed by psychologists fell from 32 percent in 1938 to 18 percent in 1987 (Ethics Committee of the American Psychological Association, 1988). Perhaps this drop reflects that government policy to protect human subjects may have succeeded in preventing research infractions common in the past.

15.1.3 Preventing Human Subject Violations: Moved by the Tuskegee Syphilis Study scandal, Congress passed the National Research Act in 1974, which led to the establishment of the National Commission on the Protection of Human Subjects of Biomedical and Behavioural Research. Its recommendations in 1978 led the Department of Health and Human Services to issue regulations finalized in 1981.

Because of the seeming inability of the legal system and professional organizations to protect human subjects, the federal government took charge of stopping harmful research practices. Because it provides a large share of the funds for social research, the government can set guidelines that can directly or indirectly influence most research. Federal regulations now require that each institution that sponsors any research funded by the Department of Health and Human Services establish local review committees to screen proposals. Even if a researcher could function without federal funds, he or she usually still needs the permission of an institution to use its facilities, subject pool, and graduate assistants.

In 1981, the current federal regulations appeared in the *Federal Register*. These guidelines define the types of prior review provided by Institutional Review Boards (IRBs). Although required only for projects with or seeking federal funds, these guidelines usually apply to all research at each institution. Each institution must state how it will review non-federally funded research shows the institution's commitment to the protection of human subjects.

Human research proposals fall into three categories of review: exempt, expedited and full. The first category, exempt, includes no or very low-risk proposals as judged by the investigators and applies to fall in the exempt category need file only an Exempt Registration Form with the IRB showing evidence that the researcher's department chair or dean has reviewed the proposed research.

Exempt studies include the following categories:

1. Research on "normal educational practices".
2. Use of educational tests, surveys, or observations unless the subjects can be identified and disclosure of their responses could harm their legal or financial standing or their reputations.
3. Use of educational tests, surveys, or observations of public behaviour not exempt under the second category if the subjects are elected or appointed public officials or candidates for public office or if federal statutes require that the confidentiality of the personally identifiable information be maintained.
4. Study of existing data if the data are publicly available or if the subjects cannot be identified.
5. Research and demonstration projects conducted by approval of federal agency heads that are designed to promote or improve public service programs.
6. Taste and food quality studies not involving addictives or with ingredients at levels found safe by federal agencies.

The option of researchers to exempt their own research from review has raised concern in those who want maximum federal protection of human subjects (Veatch, 1981). In contrasts, others have noted some types of non-exempt research that they believe should have been exempted (Thompson et al., 1981). Finally, remember that the federal procedures define a minimum level of protection to which each institution of IRB can add higher standards.

If the researcher claims no exemption, he or she must submit the research proposal for review by the IRB. Full review involves a formal evaluation by the entire IRB. A speedier form of review, called expedited review, can be conducted by a single experienced member of the IRB (for example, its chairperson). Expedited review applies to relatively low-risk research involving mainly biomedical techniques such as collecting hair, nail clippings, sweat, small amounts of blood, or dental plaque. Social research techniques considered low-risk for expedited review include non-invasive physiological recordings of adults (for example, testing sensory acuity); voice recordings; the use of existing documents; and non-stressful studies of group behaviour, perception and cognition.

Full review applies to proposals that do not fall in the exempt or expedited categories. In full review, the committee tries both to assure no excessive risk of harm and to weigh the relation of benefit to harm in the utilitarian sense. The full review judges the adequacy of the informed consent procedure and the protection of the subjects' identity were appropriate. The IRB must decide whether the subjects have the ability to give informed consent (for example, in studies using children and mentally disabled subjects) and whether the study poses any risk of concern (for example, studies of students or prisoners in a dependent relationship to the investigator) can obtain such prior consent, the standards for the procedure seem clear.

Ordinarily, the researcher should provide the prospective subject with verbal and written information about the study and a waiver form for his or her signature. The information that provides the basis for this consent usually includes the study's purpose and duration, subject confidentiality procedures, risk and benefits, whom to contact for further details, and a statement that participation is voluntary with no penalty for stopping at any time. After receiving and considering this information, the subjects can indicate their consent their consent to participate in writing. This written consent does not waive any of the subject's legal rights or release the researcher from liability for negligence in the research project.

Federal rules permit the IRBs to waive the requirement for written informed consent, but they do so reluctantly and only for very good reason. An IRB may waive informed consent when the research cannot proceed without the waiver. For example, experiments that depend on deception would not succeed if the subjects knew of the deception in advance. In some field studies, the participant observer can gain entry only by concealing his or her research role. Such studies would become impossible if prior informed consent were needed. The IRB will grant such waivers only if the risk to the subjects appears minimal and warranted by the benefits expected from the study. Usually, the researcher, in exchange for the waiver of prior consent, must provide full information to the subjects at the end of the study.

The IRBs deliberation takes place in the context of continuing debate between those who oppose deceptive research procedures on principle (Baumrind, 1985) and those who have found significant effects of such ethical requirements on research outcomes (Trice, 1987). Not surprisingly, IRB decisions have varied in response to the social sensitivity of the topic. In one survey, IRBs were more likely to reject proposals that dealt with issues such as racial or sexual discrimination (Ceci, Peters and Plotkin, 1985). Some researchers who desire more consistent IRB decisions have proposed supplying a casebook of actual research protocols to help standardize decisions over time and across different IRBs (Rosnow, Rotheram-Borus, Ceci, Blanck and Koocher, 1993).

15.2 Objectivity

Besides the concern for protecting human subjects, several other important dilemmas exists, including one that arise in socially sensitive research (Sieber and Stanley, 1988). Conflicts involving other figures in the research enterprise have led to additional guidelines. In some cases, these ethics standards elicit little controversy. For other conflicts, guidelines will continue to trigger public and professional debate.

Ethical conflicts in research derive from the variety of players and their divergent self-interests and values. The major players include the researcher, the subject, the funder, and a society as me consumer of research.

Other parties also figure in the process of science, including professional associations, scholarly journals, research institutions such as universities, and government in its regulatory role. The distinctions among these parties are not always clear-cut, since one may play two or more parts—for example, the government as funder, as consumer of research results, as regulator, and as investigator (for instance, the collection of census data). In addition, each of these players may have different priorities. Since these priorities sometimes collide, ethical problems can arise between any two parties in the research process. Competing interests may well try to achieve their aims at the expense of the other parties involved.

15.3 Research versus Researcher

15.3.1 Plagiarism: One ethical conflict raises little controversy. Virtually all professional groups prohibit plagiarism, and copyright laws provide laws for stealing another author's published writing. However, the explosive increase in scientific journals makes it difficult to catch plagiarized, especially when it is published in obscure journals. Most cases of research misconduct involve plagiarism (LaFollette, 1992). Just one plagiarist can publish dozens of articles before being caught (for example, the Al-gabti case described in Broad and Wade, 1982).

When he or she is caught, the plagiarist can suffer severe penalties. Jerri Husch, a sociologist, discovered in 1988 that large section of her 1984 Ph.D. dissertation on Musak in the workplace had appeared un-credited in a book by Stephen Barnes. Dr. Husch initiated a complaint and in 1989 a committee of the American Sociological Association concluded that Barnes had plagiarized the material. When no satisfaction was obtained from Dr. Barnes or his publisher, the organization raised the matter with Dr. Barne's employer, Eastern New Mexico University, where he worked as Dean of Fine Arts. By the end of 1989, Dr. Barnes had left his job (Buff, 1989), apparently, in part, due to this pressure.

Some plagiarism disputes are less clear-cut than using another's published work without permission. The professor who puts his or her name on a student's work shows how research can be "stolen" before the publication stage. In an era of large-scale team research, disputes can easily arise about authorship and the sharing of credit for creative contribution. Such disputes, unless prevented by agreements in the early stages of collaboration, can and do produce long-lasting hostility.

15.3.2 Peer Review of Research. In contrast to the rules against plagiarism, the ethical codes have achieved less clarity on another potential conflict between researchers. In employment and promotion decisions, reviews of papers submitted for publication, and in grant request for research funds, researchers usually receive judgments by their peers on the merits of their research. These decisions can govern which research reports will receive wide publication or none at all and which proposals will receive funding or never be carried out. Such peer review procedures require fairness and objectivity. Suspicion that the peer review mechanism is working with bias could produce interpersonal conflict between competing scholars. Possible abuses in peer review also raise concern about distortions in the substantive direction of future research as decisions favour certain types of research proposals and research careers over others.

The peer review process tries to protect itself by using multiple reviewers. But whereas lawbreakers usually have the protection of 12 member juries, professional researchers are often judged by as few as two to five peers. Research on the peer review process in awarding grants has cast serious doubt on its reliability. One research team had 150 National Science Foundation proposals re-evaluated. They conducted that "the fate of a particular grant application is roughly half determined by the elements which might be characterized as the 'luck of the reviewer draw" (Cole and Simon, 1981). Research on peer review of manuscripts submitted for publication also suggests low levels of quality and later citation (Cicchetti, 1980) and only modest relationships between peer judgments of quality and later citation (Gottfredson, 1978). However, "blind" review techniques used by many of the best journals offer some protection against sex, ethnic, or personal bias in manuscript review.

15.4 Society versus Researcher

15.4.1 Fraud. With great embarrassment, scientists have had to admit that their colleagues sometimes engage in fraud. The problem rarely involves financial fraud, looting he research grant to buy expensive cars and vacations, although perhaps that exists as well. The main problem is falsifying data. The motive to make up or trim data may derive from the desire to gain career success through publications. But the impact of such fraud goes beyond the careers of individual researchers and can reach al the way to socially significant public policy.

Cases of documented fraud, although rare historically, appear to be on the rise (Broad and Wade, 1982; LaFollette, 1992). One such case involved Stephen Breuning, a young psychologist whose research was funded by the National Institute of Mental Health (NIMH). Breuning published studies between 1980 and 1984 on the effects of psychoactive drugs on the mentally retarded. His findings influenced treatment practices in some states, including Connecticut. However, “only a few of the experimental subjects described in (some of the investigator’s) publications and progress reports were ever studied” (Hostetler, 1987). Some of the questionable reports were co-authored by respected researchers who, despite little or no involvement in the research, lent their names to the reports or whose names were added without their permission.

The NIMH investigating panel recommended that Breuning be barred from additional NIMH funding for 10 years and that the case be handed over to the Department of Justice, which subsequently indicated him, the first such indictment in federal court. His institution had to reimburse NIHM more than $ 163,000 for misspent grants (Bales, 1988). In a subsequent plea bargain, Breuning pleaded guilty, becoming a subject to a minimum penalty of 10 years in prison and $ 20,000 in fines. His actual sentences consisted of 60 days in a halfway house, 250 hours of community service, and 5 years of probation. We may never know the extent of harm done to retarded patients whose treatment was guided by these fraudulent findings. A citation study did track the number of research studies that cited 20 of Breuning's questionable reports (Garfield and Welljams-Dorof, 1990). Out of 200 citations, 80 (40 percent) were self-citations by Breuning or his co-author. Non-self-citations fell after 1986 when the scandal broke and reflected little apparent impact of his claims.

15.4.2 Burt Case: Fraud or Politics: The most famous case of alleged fraud in the social sciences involves Sir Cyril Burt. He died a greatly esteemed scholar in 1971, once called the "dean of the world's psychologists" (Dreger, quoted by Hearnshaw, 1979). Burl co-founded the *British Journal of Statistical Psychology* in 1947 and controlled or helped control it until 1963. He studied the source of intelligence—genetic inheritance or rearing and the environment—using identical twins. Identical twins usually score the same in intelligence tests. Because most twins grow up in the same environment as well as sharing the same genes, we cannot tell which source causes the similarity. However, identical twins reared apart have the same genes but grow up in different environments. Scholars who think environmental causes intelligence would expect to score low correlations between the intelligence scores of twins reared apart. Those who believe that genes cause intelligence expect high correlations regardless of environmental differences in rearing. Burt claimed to have found more identical twins reared apart than anyone else in the intelligence area—15 such sets in 1943, 21 by 1955, twice that number in 1958, and 53 in his last report of 1966.

Burt reported high correlations (typically, 77) supporting the genetic heritability of intelligence. These findings served as the basis for Burt's defence of British educational policy, which then selected children into higher and lower tracks based on early tests. They also figured in the volatile debate about the relation of race and intelligence. Burt's work roused great animosity from both other psychologists and people in political circles. However, his great stature protected him from charges of fraud until after his death. The first doubt about his work arose from the incredible consistency of his reports, which repeatedly gave the same correlation for intelligence of twins reared apart.

Another question concerned publications in Burt's journal on his data by two authors named Howard and Conway. A report named Oliver Gillie of the London Times tried to contact them in 1976 to get their views of Burt's data. Not able to locate them, he charged that Burt had written the papers himself and assigned authorship to nonexistent people. Other scholars who disliked Burt's genetic views on intelligence added their weight to the charges that Burt had falsified his data. When Hearnshaw, a respected biographer, concluded that Burt has committed fraud, the case seemed closed on the greatest scandal in the history of social science (1979).

In the late 1980s, two independent scholars, with no stake in the genetic versus environment debate, reviewed the Burt case (Fletcher, 1991; Joyson, 1989). They converged on a view that partially exonerates Burt and charges his accusers with character defamation. Burt clearly engaged in misconduct by writing and publishing the papers attributed to Howard and Conway. However, these individuals existed and served as unsalaried social workers who helped Burt with his data collection in the 1920s and 1930s. The lapse in time explains the difficulty Gillie had in finding them. Burt's action in assigning them the authorships may have been his misguided way of giving them the credit for their help. As for the identical correlations, it now appears that Burt was simply carrying over findings reported in one article to later articles and not claiming new computations with the same results. The best check on Burt's claims comes from other independent research.

At least two separate studies of identical twins reared apart have reported intelligence correlations of .77, exactly the same as Burt (Jensen, 1992). Apparently, both the media and psychologists in leadership positions wrongly accused Burt in order to impugn his views on the heritability of intelligence. In so doing, they not only smeared a leading scholar after he could no longer defend himself, but they cast doubt on the methods he had helped pioneer, such as measurement of mental abilities.

15.4.3 Waste: We can think of fraud as a special case of waste in which research funds have disappeared without return of valid results. Another kind of waste can occur when no fraud takes place. An instance of this conflict between funder and researchers appears in the Hutchinson versus Proxmire case (Kielsler and Lowman, 1980). Senator Proxmire waged a campaign to save taxpayers' money from being wasted on trivial research. He publicized extreme cases of such alleged waste with his Golden Fleece Award. Ronald Hutchinson received this embarrassing award in 1975 for his work on aggression in monkeys. Proxmire took credit for stopping Hutchinson's federal funding, and Hutchinson sued Proxmire. The Supreme Court ruled in favour of Hutchinson's claim that he was not a public figure subject to Proxmire's public ridicule and remanded the suit back to a lower court. Proxmire then settled out of court in 1980 for a public apology and US$ 10,000.

Although Dr. Hutchinson won the battle, Senator Proxmire may have won the war. The chilling effect of public ridicule and the power of lawmakers to restrict public research funds surely have an impact on what researchers can explore with public support. No professional association's ethical guidelines define what "significant" social research is. Presumably, individual professionals have freedom to pursue their curiosity. Indeed, an honoured intellectual tradition supports pure or basic research for it s own sake regardless of its potential uses. On the other, the taxpayers' representatives have an obligation to spend scarce public funds wisely.

The allocation of research must, therefore, take into account the welfare of the entire society and not just the curiosity of researchers. But how should the conflict between the researcher's interests and the social interests be resolved? Researchers often claim that it is short-sighted to limit support to applied research. Since applied research depends on theory and pure research, it will wither in the future if the funders stifle the curiosity of the pure researchers now. On the other hand, we must seek the best possible uses of our scarce research funds and thus pay special attention to our funding priorities (Boulding, 1966).

But if politicians grand us from trivial research, who guards against their awarding research grants in their own or other special interests? Awarding government research funds by peer review (juries of fellow scientists) gives no guarantee that funds will spread evenly across congregational districts. Increasingly, lawmakers are pork-barreling research grants to provide jobs in the home states and districts (Clifford, 1987). In one instance, a Massachusetts politician took credit for getting a US$ 7.7 million research centre for his home district. This occurred over the advice of a technical review panel, which favoured another bidder, whose proposal would have cost the taxpayers US$ 3.2 million less (Cordes, 1984). Professional research associations lobby the government to increase the funds put into their fields of interest. Universities and private companies also lobby Congress to give funds outside of the usual peer review process for special interest projects. The value of such "earmarked" projects by Congress increased 70-fold between 1980 and 1992 (Agnew, 1993).

15.5 Public Interest versus Private Interest

Science operates within and reflects society. Science, wittingly or not, often carries out the values of the society, or at least that part of society from which scientists come. That scientists see reality through the blinders of society's values, cause concern for those who want science to understand society to make it better. Collecting the data within the political and economic status quo will prove irrelevant, it is argued, for the goal of seeing beyond the status quo to a different future (Sarason, 1981).

15.5.1 Private Interests: In a complex society, no single homogenous value set exists from which everyone approaches political and social problems. Rather, we find many competing private interests. The government may reflect those private interests that were on the winning side of the last election or coup. Thus, research funded in one administration may be eliminated by the next administrator. Just as the government can support research with its funds outside of peer review, it can cut off funding that has earned peer review approval. This can happen when the research topic touches a political nerve. For example, in September 1992, the National Institute of Health withdrew previously approved funds for a University of Maryland conference on ethical issues related to genetic studies of crime. Opponents of the conference feared that this research would try to link violence to race. Proponents viewed the withdrawal of funds as bureaucratic cowardice in the face of pressure for political correctness (Touchett, 1992). The fear raised by this conference shows the distrust that many hold that science might be used to harm an ethnic or racial group.

A more clear-cut type of private interest is the corporation that can sponsor research to serve its own ends. For example, a tobacco firm may fund research on public attitudes towards smoking prohibition (for example, to prevent laws that outlaw smoking in restaurants). Naturally, the funder has a vested interest in finding techniques that would increase profits by blocking the adoption of such laws. What effect does this natural self-interest have on the researchers' effort? To what extent should such privately employed researchers concern themselves with the "public interest"?

In recognition of this potential conflict, professional associations have provided guidelines regarding research sponsorship. For example, the Code of Ethics of the American

Sociological Association calls for identification of all sources of all sources of research support or special relationships with sponsors (American Sociological Association, 1989). Similarly, the anthropologists' Statement of Ethics warns that in "working for governmental or private businesses, anthropologists should be especially careful not to promise or imply acceptance of conditions contrary to professional ethics or competing commitments" (Council of American Anthropological Association, 1990).

In recent years, universities have begun to add force to such requirements. Professors often must report their link with private industry and their funding from non-public sources. Such reporting permits an assessment of possible conflict of interest, and local boards can provide peer review and guidance in questionable cases.

15.5.2 Public Interest: Although conflicts involving special interests may seem clear enough, identifying the public interest appears much more difficult. What if the public interest of a nation supported social research that was, arguably, unethical? A notorious example of this kind of research appeared in Project Camelot (Horowitz, 1973), a study that gauged the causes of revolutions in the Third World. Supported by the U.S. military, it sought techniques for avoiding or coping with revolutions. Survey and other methods were to be used in various developing countries after Camelot's conception in 1963.

The uproar over Camelot ignited when a Chilean sociology professor challenged the military implications of the project. The Chilean press and the Chilean senate viewed Camelot as espionage. This criticism resulted in U.S. congressional hearings and the termination of Camelot by the Defence Department in August 1965.

With respect to such research projects as Camelot, Beals (1969) asks "whether social science should be the handmaiden of government or strife for freedom and autonomy". Since the "true" public interest may be in the eye of the beholder, a resolution of this matter will not be simple. Given the increasing importance of science in public policy and social welfare, scientists bear an increasing responsibility to consider the consequences of their work. Just how to consider the long-run consequences and how to weigh the potentially different effects on different sections of society (for example, poor versus rich within a society or First World versus Third World motions) has not been worked out in any laws or professional codes. Perhaps for that reason, the movement of "public interest science" will continue as an educational and consciousness-raising force before it can be formulated by consensus.

15.5.3 Protecting Research Integrity: In response to the subject of protecting human subjects, the government created preventive procedures such as IRBs for screening research proposals. However, no similar system exists for preventing other kind of research misconduct such as plagiarism or fraud. At best, individual whistle-blowers can raise charges when they spot such abuses.

15.5.4 Legal Remedies. Of course, an author can seek legal address in cases of plagiarism upon finding that someone has published his or her words without proper credit. Such actions can proceed under the copyrighted work. A more recent law permits legal action in cases of fraud that wastes public funds.

Under the False Claim Amendment Act of 1986, any individual can bring suit, on behalf of the United States, in a federal district court to recover funds fraudulently paid to contractors or grantees. The Department of Justice may or may not choose to join such suits. But the whistle-blower who brings such a suite may receive a reward up to 30 percent of triple the damages suffered by the government as a result of the researcher's fraud (Charrow and Saks, 1992). Thus, if you believe that a researcher is making up data and misspending a government grant, you can take him or her to court and earn a reward for your trouble if you prevail.

15.5.5 Institutional Hearings: Ideally, researchers will avoid misconduct if they know the rules of proper research. Government research agencies, under congressional pressure, have tried to spell out and enforce rules for research integrity. For example, the Public Health Service now has an Office of Research Integrity (ORI), which proposes guidelines for misconduct (for example, prohibiting plagiarism or making up data).

However, when charges of misconduct arise, we must have a means for judging them. The government now expects each research institution to establish its own office of scientific integrity to disseminate the rules of proper research and to judge infractions reported locally. For example, the research integrity office of the University of Pittsburgh handled the Needleman case. Thus, if you suspect that a researcher on your campus has committed misconduct, you can report it to your local office of research integrity. There you should find established procedures for investigating and judging your complaint.

These procedures should help not only the whistle-blower; they should also provide some protection for the accused against loss of reputation to false complaints. Because these research integrity offices have appeared on many college campuses only in recent years, some are still working out their procedures. We can expect that some cases (for example, Needleman's) will continue on from theses local jurisdictions into the courts or the federal Office of Research Integrity before final resolution. Ultimately, if the federal Office of Research Integrity decides that a researcher has engaged in misconduct, it could withhold future funding as punishment.

Bibliography

Bibliography

Ackoff, Russell L., Scientific Method, New York: John Wiley and Sons, 1962.

Ackoff, Russell L., The Design of Social Research, Chicago: University of Chicago Press, 1961.

Alan Bryman, Barriers to Integrating Quantitative and Qualitative Research, *Journal of Mixed Methods Research*, Sage Publications.

Alan Bryman, Integrating Quantitative and Qualitative Research: How is it Done?, Volume 6 (1), 97-113, University of Leicester, Sage Publications, 2006.

Allen, T. Harrell, New Methods in Social Science Research, New York: Praeger Publishers, 1978.

Anderson, H. H., and Anderson, G. L., An Introduction to Projective Techniques and Other Devices for Understanding the Dynamics of Human Behaviour, New York: Prentice Hall, 1951.

Anderson, T.W., An Introduction to Multivariate Analysis, New York: John Wiley and Sons, 1958.

Bell, J.E., Projective Techniques: A Dynamic Approach to the Study of Personality, New York: Longmans Green, 1948.

Bellenger, Danny N., and Greenberg, Barnett A., Marketing Research: A Management Information Approach, Homewood, Illinois: Richard D. Irwin, Inc., 1978.

Bhattacharya, Srinibas, Psychdmetrics and Behavioural Research, New Delhi: Sterling Publishers Pvt. Ltd., 1972.

Boot, John C.G., and Cox, Edwin B., Statistical Analysis for Managerial Decisions, 2nd ed., New Delhi: McGraw-Hill Publishing Co. Ltd., (International Student Edition), 1979.

Bowley, A.L., Elements of Statistics, 6th ed. London: P.S. King and Staples Ltd., 1937.

Burgess, Ernest W., "Research Methods in Sociology", in Georges Gurvitch and W.E. Moore (ed.), Twentieth Century Sociology, New York: New York Philosophical Library, 1949.

Chance, William A., Statistical Methods for Decision Making, Bombay; D.B. Taraporevala Sons and Co. Pvt. Ltd., 1975.

Chaturvedi, J.C., Mathematical Statistics, Agra: Nok Jhonk Karyalaya, 1953.

Clover, Vernon T., and Balsley, Howard L., Business Research Methods, Columbus, O.: Grid, Inc., 1974.

Cochran, W.G., Sampling Techniques, 2nd ed., New York: John Wiley and Sons, 1963.

Cooley, William W., and Lohnes, Paul R., Multivariate Data Analysis, New York: John Wiley and Sons, 1971.

Dass, S.L., Personality Assessment through Projective Movie Pictures, New Delhi: S. Chand and Co. Pvt. Ltd., 1974.

Davis, G.B., Introduction to Computers, 3rd ed., McGraw-Hill International Book Co., 1981.

Deming, W. Edwards, Sample Design in Business Research, New York: John Wiley and Sons, 1960.

Dennis, Child, The Essentials of Factor Analysis, New York: Holt, Rinehart and Winston, 1973.

Denzin, Norman, The Research Act, Chicago: Aldine, 1973.

Edwards, Allen L., Techniques of Attitude Scale Construction, New York: Appleton-Century-Crofts, 1957.

Edwards, Allen, Statistical Methods, 2nd ed., New York: Holt, Rinehart and Winston, 1967.

Emory, C. William, Business Research Methods, Illinois: Richard D. Irwin, Inc., Homewood, 1976.

Ferber, Robert (ed.), Handbook of Marketing Research, New York: McGraw-Hill, Inc., 1948.

Festinger, Leon and Katz, Daniel (eds.), Research Methods in Behavioural Sciences, New Delhi: Amerind Publishing Co. Pvt. Ltd., Fourth Indian Reprint, 1976.

Fiebleman, J.K., Scientific Methods, Netherlands: Martinus Nijhoff, The Hague, 1972.

Fisher, R.A., Statistical Methods for Research Workers, 13th ed., New York: Hafner Publishing Co., 1958.

Fruchter, Benjamin, Introduction to Factor Analysis, Princeton, N.J.: D. Van Nostrand, 1954.

Gatner, Elliot S.M., and Cordasco, Francesco, Research and Report Writing, New York: Barnes and Noble Inc., 1956.

Gaum, Carl G., Graves, Harod F., and Hoffman, Lyne, S.S., Report Writing, 3rd ed., New York: Prentice-Hall, 1950.

Ghosh, B.N., Scientific Methods and Social Research, New Delhi: Sterling Publishers Pvt. Ltd., 1982.

Gibbons, J.D., Nonparametric Statistical Inference, Tokyo: McGraw-Hill Kogakusha Ltd., (International Student Edition), 1971.

Giles, G.B., Marketing, 2nd ed., London: Macdonald and Evans Ltd., 1974.

Glock, Charles Y., Survey Research in the Social Sciences, New York: Russell Sage Foundation, 1967.

Godfrey, Arthur, Quantitative Methods for Managers, London: Edward Arnold (Publishers) Ltd., 1977.

Gorden, Raymond L., Interviewing: Strategy, Techniques and Tactics, rev. ed., Homewood, 111: Dorsey Press, 1975.

Green, Paul E., Analyzing Multivariate Data, Hinsdale, 111: Dryden Press, 1978.

Green, Paul E., and Carmone, F.J., Multidimensional Scaling in Marketing Analysis, Boston: Allyn and Bacon, Inc., 1970.

Guilford, J.P., Psychometric Methods, New York: McGraw-Hill, Inc., 1954.

Harnett, Donald L., and Murphy, James L., Introductory Statistical Analysis, Philippines: Addison-Wesley Publishing Co. Inc., 1975.

Husain, S. Sociology, Trueman's Specific Series, Danika Publishing Company, New Delhi, 2012.

Hyman, Herbert H., et al., Interviewing in Social Research, Chicago: University of Chicago Press, 1975.

Isha Ray, Designing Social Research: Key Elements. MSRI-IISc Summer School, June 17, 2010.

John, Peter W. M., Statistical Design and Analysis of Experiments, New York: The Macmillan Co., 1971.

Johnson, Ellen, The Research Report: A Guide for the Beginner, New York: Ronald Press, 1951.

Johnson, Rodney D., and Siskin, Bernard R., Quantitative Techniques for Business Decisions, New Delhi: Prentice-Hall of India Pvt. Ltd., 1977.

Kerlinger, Fred N. and Pedhazur, Elazar J., Multiple Regression in Behavioural Research, New York: Holt, Rinehart and Winston, 1973.

Kerlinger, Fred N., Foundations of Behavioural Research, 2nd ed., New York: Holt, Reinhart and Winston, 1973.

Kish, Leslie, Survey Sampling, New York: John Wiley and Sons, Inc., 1965.

Kothari, C.R., Quantitative Techniques, 2nd ed., New Delhi: Vikas Publishing House Pvt. Ltd., 1984.

Lastrucci, Carles L., The Scientific Approach: Basic Principles of the

Scientific Method, Cambridge, Mass.: Schenkman Publishing Co., Inc., 1967.

Levine, S. and Elzey, Freeman F., A Programmed Introduction to Research, California: Woods Worth Publishing Co., 1968.

Maranell, Gary M. (ed.), Scaling: A Source Book for Behavioural Scientists, Chicago: Aldine, 1974.

Maxwell, Albert E., Analyzing Qualitative Data, New York: John Wiley and Sons, 1961.

Meir, Robert C., Newell, William T. and Dazier, Harold L., Simulation in Business and Economics, Englewood Cliffs, N.J.: Prentice Hall, Inc., 1969.

Miller, Delbert C., Handbook of Research Design and Social Measurement, 3rd ed., New York: David Mckay Company, Inc., 1977.

Morrison, Donald F., Multivariate Statistical Methods, New York: McGraw-Hill, 1967.

Nagel, Stuart S., and Neef, Marian, Policy Analysis in Social Science Research, London: Sage Publications, 1979.

Nie, N. H., Bent, D. H., and Hull, C. H., Statistical Package for the Social Sciences, New York: McGraw-Hill, 1970.

Noether, G.E., Elements of Nonparametric Statistics, New York: John Wiley and Sons, Inc., 1967.

Nunnally, Jum C., Psychometric Theory, 2nd ed., New York: McGraw-Hill, 1978.

Odum, H.W., and Jocher, Katharine, An Introduction to Social Research, New York: Henry Holt and Co., 1929.

Oppenheim, A. N., Questionnaire Design and Attitude Measurement, New York: Basic Books, 1966.

Ostle, Bernard, and Mensing, Richard W., Statistics in Research, 3rd ed., Ames Iowa: The Iowa State University Press, 1975.

Payne, Stanley, The Art of Asking Questions, Princeton: Princeton University Press, 1951.

R., Chandrasekhar, How to Write a Thesis: A Working Guide, Australian Research Centre for Medical Engineering (ARCME), The University of Western Australia, 2000.

Rajaraman, V., Fundamentals of Computers, New Delhi: Prentice-Hall of India Pvt. Ltd., 1985.

Ramchandran, P., Training in Research Methodology in Social Sciences in India, New Delhi: ICSSR 1971.

Robert F. Wagner, Sonia Ospina, Qualitative Research, Encyclopedia of

Leadership, Edited by G. Goethals, G. Sorenson, J. MacGregor, Sage Publications, 2004.

Roscoe, John T., Fundamental Research Statistics for the Behavioural Sciences, New York: Holt, Rinehart and Winston, Inc., 1969.

Runyon, Richard P., Inferential Statistics, Philippines: Addison-Wesley Publishing Company, Inc., 1977.

Sadhu, A.N., and Singh, Amarjit, Research Methodology in Social Sciences, Bombay: Himalaya Publishing House, 1980.

Seboyar, G.E., Manual for Report and Thesis Writing, New York: F.S. Crofts and Co., 1929.

Selltiz, Claire, Jahoda, Marie, Deutsch, Morton, and Cook, Stuart W., Research Methods in Social Relations, rev. ed. New York: Holt, Rinehart and Winston, Inc., 1959.

Takeuchi, K., Yanai, H. and Mukherjee, B.N., The Foundations of Multivariate Analysis, New Delhi: Wiley Eastern Ltd., 1982.

Tandon, B.C., Research Methodology in Social Sciences, Allahabad: Chaitanya Publishing House, 1979.

Thorndike, Robert L. and Hagen, Elizabeth P., Measurement and Evaluation in Psychology and Education, 4th ed., New York: John Wiley and Sons, 1977.

Thurstone, L.L., The Measurement of Values, Chicago: University of Chicago Press, 1959.

Tim, May, Social Research Issues, Methods and Process, Open University Press Buckingham, Philadelphia, 2001.

Torgerson, W., Theory and Methods of Scaling, New York: John Wiley and Sons, 1958.

Travers, Robert M. W, An Introduction to Educational Research, 4th ed., New York: Macmillan Publishing Co., Inc., 1978.

Tryon, R.C., and Bailey, D.E., Cluster Analysis, New York: McGraw-Hill, 1970.

Ullman, Neil R., Elementary Statistics, New York: John Wiley and Sons Inc., 1978.

Whitney, F.L., The Elements of Research, 3rd ed., New York: Prentice-Hall, 1950.

Wilkinson, T.S. and Bhandarkar, P.L., Methodology and Techniques of Social Research, Bombay: Himalaya Publishing House, 1979.

Willemsen, Eleanor Walker, Understanding Statistical Reasoning, San Francisco: W.H. Freeman and Company, 1974.

Yamane, T., Statistics: An Introductory Analysis, 3rd ed., New York: Harper and Row, 1973.

Young, Pauline V., Scientific Social Surveys and Research, 3rd ed., New York: Prentice-Hall, 1960.

Bibliography

Index

Index